New Mexico

NEW MEXICO BY ROAD

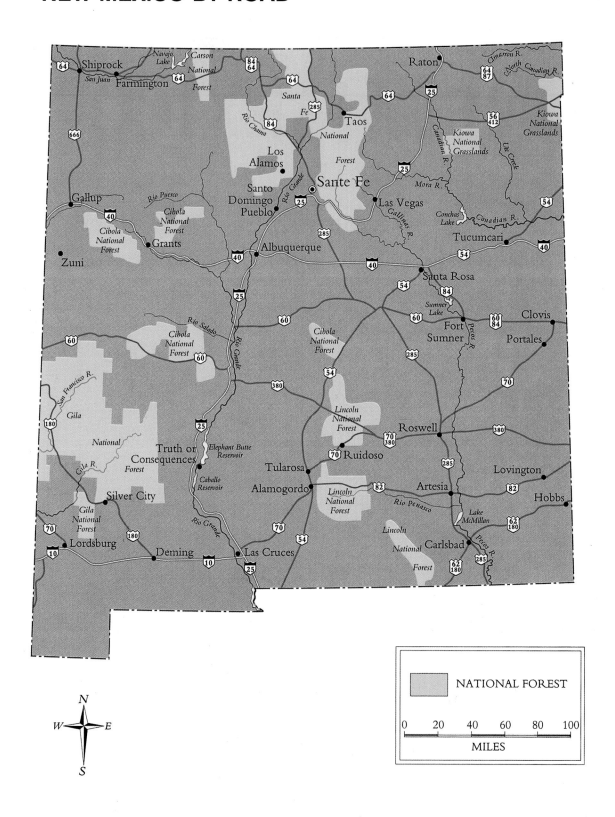

NATIONAL FOREST

0   20   40   60   80   100
MILES

N
W   E
S

Celebrate the States

New Mexico

Melissa McDaniel, Ettagale Blauer, and Jason Lauré

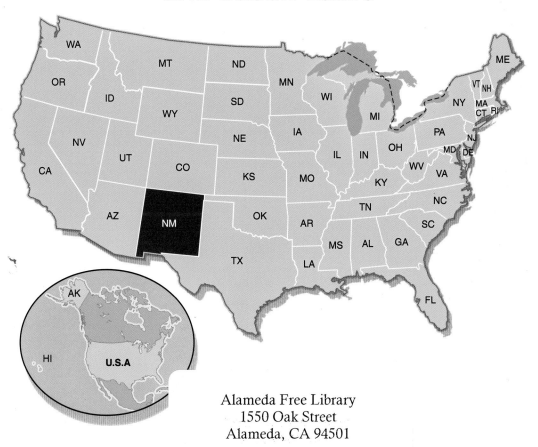

Alameda Free Library
1550 Oak Street
Alameda, CA 94501

Marshall Cavendish
Benchmark
New York

Marshall Cavendish Benchmark
99 White Plains Road
Tarrytown, NY 10591-9001
www.marshallcavendish.us

All Internet addresses were correct and accurate at the time of printing.

Library of Congress Cataloging-in-Publication Data
McDaniel, Melissa, 1964–
New Mexico / by Melissa McDaniel, Ettagale Blauer, and Jason Lauré. — 2nd ed.
p. cm. — (Celebrate the states)
Summary: "Provides comprehensive information on the geography, history, wildlife, governmental
structure, economy, cultural diversity, peoples, religion, and landmarks of
New Mexico"—Provided by publisher.
Includes bibliographical references and index.
ISBN 978-0-7614-2719-3
1. New Mexico—Juvenile literature. I. Blauer, Ettagale. II. Lauré, Jason. III. Title. IV. Series.
F796.3.M34 2008
972—dc22
2007009273

Editor: Christine Florie
Publisher: Michelle Bisson
Art Director: Anahid Hamparian
Series Designer: Adam Mietlowski

Photo research by Connie Gardner

Cover photo by Tim Fitzharris/Minden Pictures/Getty Images

The photographs in this book are used by permission and through the courtesy of: *Corbis:* Richard
Cummins, back cover; Adam Woodfit, 13; David Muench, 15, 96; Mark Gibson, 25; Macduff Everton,
26, 120; George H. Huey, 30, 98, 107, 109; Bettmann, 34, 45. 46. 49; Academy of National Sciences of
Philadelphia, 37; Bob Krist, 52, 57; Danny Lehman, 55, 83; Richard T. Norwitz, 67, 81; Steven
Clevenger, 72, 88; Peter Tunley, 75; Tom Bean, 77; Craig Aurness, 78; James Marshall, 84; Blaine
Harrington, 90, 111; Kevin Fleming, 99, 101; David Houser, 105, 128; Corbis, 127; Reuters, 131;
Frank Trapper, 133; *PhotoEdit:* Spencer Grant, 68; *Alamy:* Greg Vaughn, 8; Tom Mackie, 12; Tom Till,
18; M.L. Pearson, 41; Digital Focus, 73; Ernesto Burciaga, 86; Steve Hamblin, 106; Picpics, 111
(Bottom); *SuperStock:* age footstock, 11, 111 (Top), 115; Jack Novak, 48; *Getty:* Altrendo, 17, 92;
Hulton Archive, 32; Phillippe Diederich, 64; Chip Somodevilla, 65; National Geographic, 95; Image
Bank, 125; Steve Snowden, 126; Science Faction, 137; *Dembinsky Photo Associates:* Stan Osolinski, 22;
Minden Pictures: Tim Fitzharris, 19; Gerry Ellis, 21; *Art Resource:* Smithsonian American Art Museum,
Washington DC, 28; *North Wind Picture Archive:* 38, 39, 40; *The Image Works:* Jack Kurtz, 51; Jeff
Greenberg, 54; Andre Jenny, 59; Lisa Law, 61; Joe Sohm, 123; *AP Photo:* Marla Brose, 62.

Printed in Malaysia
1 3 5 6 4 2

Contents

New Mexico Is . . .

New Mexico is stunning landscape . . .

"The scenery is so beautiful, I have to face the wall in order to concentrate on my writing."

—author Judy Blume

"[It] is a perfectly mad looking country—hills and cliffs and washes too crazy to imagine all thrown up in the air by God and let tumble where they would."

—artist Georgia O'Keeffe

. . . under extraordinary sky.

"There was so much sky, more than at sea, more than anywhere else in the world. . . . Even the mountains were made ant-hills under it. Elsewhere the sky is the roof of the world; but here the earth was the floor of the sky."

—novelist Willa Cather

New Mexico is captivating.

"Here . . . everything was intensified for one—sight, sound, and taste—and I felt that perhaps I was more awake and more aware than I had ever been before."

—arts patron Mabel Dodge Luhan

"The moment I saw the brilliant, proud morning shine high over the deserts of Santa Fe, something stood still in my soul, and I started to attend."

—writer D. H. Lawrence

A century ago, many visitors found New Mexico a strange and exotic land.

"Before I had gone six blocks up the narrow crooked streets lined with low adobes, I began to doubt that I was in the United States of America."

—Clyde Kluckhohn, visitor in the 1920s

New Mexico's Native Americans maintain a strong link to the past.

"It brings honor and prestige to the participants who go back home and say that they competed in the Gathering of Nations."

—Ralph Zotigh, member of the drum group Zotigh Singers

New Mexico is the most foreign and the most American of all the fifty states. It is one of the most ancient places and at the same time one of the most futuristic. Cowboys and ranchers share the state with people building a spaceport. Three cultures come together here: Native Americans, Hispanics, and Anglos, the local term for nonethnic whites. In one day in Albuquerque, you can experience the tremendous chasm that exists between these three groups as well as the ways in which they interact. New Mexico is a state of extreme beauty. It is a quiet beauty that echoes the colors of the desert landscape. It is easy for a visitor to understand why New Mexico is called the Land of Enchantment.

Chapter One

Earth and Sky

New Mexico's physical appearance can strike you as rather beige, at first glance. The state does have great stretches of dry, brown, dusty earth. But that is just the background for its fascinating red-rock formations. It sets the scene for the rugged mountains that jut up into the stunning sky. The landscape does make you work a little to get to know it, but that's a small price to pay for the constantly changing views brought about by the magical light that is the essence of New Mexico. Although there is plenty of wildlife in New Mexico, it, too, requires some work on the part of the visitor. Wildlife hides in the mountains and in burrows, escaping the harsh midday sun. New Mexico's land, people, and wildlife may seem modest in appearance, but they are beautiful and powerful in their impact. What seems like an empty landscape is really a magical land waiting to be discovered. Scarcely anyone comes to New Mexico without falling in love with the land, the people, and the air.

New Mexico's High Desert Trail System is a great way to explore New Mexico's rugged terrain.

MOUNTAINS, DESERTS, AND PLAINS

New Mexico has some of the most varied landscape in the United States. In its southwestern corner, jagged mountain ranges alternate with dry desert regions. You can drive across miles of flat, dry land, then suddenly see sharp mountain spires looming ahead. As you ascend the steep roads, the temperature drops quickly, and the desert landscape gives way to lush ponderosa pine and Douglas fir trees.

While the mountain forests offer a cool retreat from New Mexico's parched land, the arid regions are just as beautiful and interesting. In some places scrubby creosote bushes dot the land so evenly that they look like they were planted that way. The deserts are particularly striking in the spring, when plants burst into bloom. Bright yellow flowers sprout from the tops of the flat, round prickly pear cactus branches. The long ocotillo stems come alive with red blossoms. The bloom of the yucca, New Mexico's state flower, is spectacular. From the middle of its circle of pointed fronds, a stalk shoots 5 feet into the air, topped with a huge constellation of white flowers.

The eastern third of New Mexico is part of the Great Plains, the rolling grasslands that stretch from North Dakota to Texas. The section of the plains along New Mexico's eastern edge is some of the flattest land on Earth. This region, called the Llano Estacado, or Staked Plain, stretches into the Texas Panhandle. In this barren land there are no hills and no trees, nothing but scrubby grass. The Llano Estacado may have been named by early European travelers who pounded stakes into the ground to show the direction they had come from—otherwise they would have lost their way because the landscape looked exactly the same in every direction.

Although many people find the Llano Estacado dull and oppressive, some who live and work there revel in its emptiness. The only dwelling

Yuccas bloom in White Sands National Monument.

on a ranch owned by one elderly couple is a hut with no running water. Yet they stay on the land. "I like the peace and quiet," the woman says.

Northwestern New Mexico contains some of the state's most dramatic landscapes. Craggy mesas and abrupt bluffs are scattered across the dusty plains. In many places soft sandstone has worn away over thousands of years, leaving odd forms. One of the most amazing areas is the Bisti Badlands, a region of twisting pillars and mushroom-shaped formations set among colorful cliffs. Walking among the bizarre spires feels like being on another planet.

Strange and bizarre rock formations make up the landscape of the Bisti Badlands.

In north-central New Mexico lie the Jemez and the Sangre de Cristo mountains, the two southernmost ranges of the Rocky Mountains. Their steep slopes are dotted with rocky outcrops and ponderosa pine, spruce, and aspen trees. The Sangre de Cristo, which means "blood of Christ" in Spanish, were named for the reddish color they turn as the day's light wanes. Writer Bill Bryson says these mountains "are just sensational . . . especially at sunset when they simply glow, as if lit from within, like jack-o'-lanterns."

Flowing between the two ranges is the Rio Grande, New Mexico's backbone. This river runs all the way down the middle of the state, from Colorado to just south of Las Cruces, before curving east to become the border between Texas and Mexico. Native Americans built their villages along the Rio Grande, as did European settlers. As the largest river in a state where riverbeds often run dry, the Rio Grande brings life.

The Rio Grande winds for part of its course through New Mexico.

LAND AND WATER

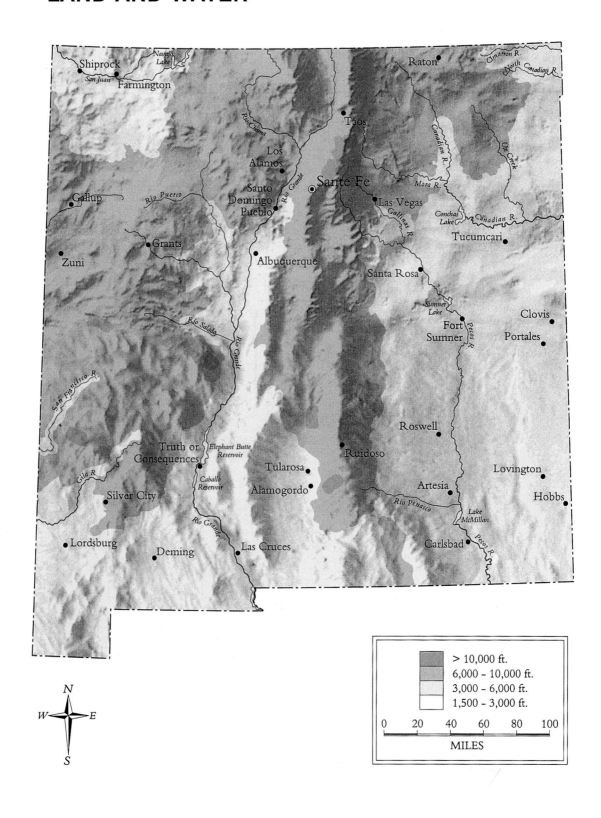

Shiprock
Navajo Lake
Raton
Cimarron R.
North Canadian R.
San Juan
Farmington
Rio Chama
Taos
Canadian R.
Ute Creek
Los Alamos
Santo Domingo Pueblo
Rio Grande
Sante Fe
Mora R.
Gallup
Rio Puerco
Las Vegas
Conchas Lake
Canadian R.
Gallinas R.
Grants
Albuquerque
Tucumcari
Zuni
Santa Rosa
Sumner Lake
Clovis
Rio Salado
Fort Sumner
Pecos R.
Portales
Rio Grande
San Francisco R.
Roswell
Truth or Consequences
Elephant Butte Reservoir
Ruidoso
Lovington
Caballo Reservoir
Tularosa
Artesia
Hobbs
Gila R.
Silver City
Alamogordo
Rio Penasco
Lake McMillan
Rio Grande
Lordsburg
Deming
Las Cruces
Carlsbad
Pecos R.

> 10,000 ft.
6,000 – 10,000 ft.
3,000 – 6,000 ft.
1,500 – 3,000 ft.

0   20   40   60   80   100
MILES

N
W   E
S

THE ENDLESS SKY

New Mexico's landscape is much more than mountains, rivers, and deserts. What lures visitors back time and again is the sky. On the state's vast flatlands, where nothing blocks the view, the sky seems larger than it does elsewhere. Even in the mountains, where the horizon is not as distant, the sky captivates. "Everyone always talks about the sky around Taos, and it is astonishing," Bryson once remarked. "I had never seen a sky so vivid and blue, so liquid."

The quality of the light and the intensity of the colors make New Mexico's sky unique. "It's the most beautiful sky in the world," said one woman who moved to New Mexico. "It makes you dream. It's like a movie, always changing. It has wonderful colors, and you can lose yourself in the openness."

New Mexico's sunsets are known for their beauty.

At night the sky is equally bewitching. Many parts of New Mexico are far from any city lights, so after nightfall countless stars are visible in the clear, dark skies.

SUN AND SNOW

New Mexico's climate is as varied as its landforms. More than 25 feet of snow fall each year in some mountainous areas, while the state's desert regions receive only a few inches of rain. Where rain does fall, it often comes in downpours in the summer during violent afternoon thunderstorms. These storms sometimes dump so much water that the parched earth cannot absorb it all. Instead the water courses over the land in dangerous flash floods.

Much of New Mexico is known for its pleasant climate. Days are warm and dry, nights cool and comfortable. Southern New Mexico's mild winters have prompted many people to retire there. Even in January towns such as Roswell reach an average high of 56 degrees Fahrenheit. During the summer the southeastern corner of the state can be scorching. After the sun sets, however, the temperature quickly drops.

In the north, winter lasts more than half the year. One disgruntled early traveler wrote that New Mexico's climate is "eight months of winter and four months of hell." But while winters are long and cold, they are also bright and sunny. In Santa Fe the sun shines more than three hundred days a year. Blinding snowstorms are often followed by dazzling blue skies, creating a lovely, sparkling landscape.

When snow does come, it can bring the whole state to a standstill. That's what happened in 2006, just two days before residents were to celebrate the New Year's holiday. A record-setting snowstorm fell over New Mexico, with the northern and central areas receiving more than 3 feet.

Fresh snow sits on the pines in the Sangre de Cristo Mountains.

The airport at Albuquerque reported a record snowfall even before the snow stopped falling. About 2 feet of snow fell in the Albuquerque metropolitan area.

In Santa Fe County more than 2 feet of snow blanketed the region. According to a report in *The New Mexican*, a local newspaper, "When Santa Fe County resident Maria Margarita Maranon realized she was stuck in her home Friday morning, it wasn't the rising snow depth, the lack of power or the fact that all her firewood was buried beneath a blanket of snow that scared her. It was the mountain lions." Maranon thought she could dig herself out but she sank into the soft, fluffy snow, up to her chest.

"I became very concerned about the mountain lions that have been coming close to my house. I didn't want to be like Little Red Riding Hood on her way to grandmother's house," she said.

When spring finally comes, it brings spectacular wildflower displays and strong winds. The wind picks up speed moving across New Mexico's unbroken expanses, keeping the Southwest's famous tumbleweeds bobbing along until they pile up against fences and buildings. Because the state is so dry and dusty, the wind causes unusual problems. Instead of warning travelers about possible ice on the road, some New Mexico highways have signs warning of dust storms.

Springtime in New Mexico brings hundreds of wildflowers.

WILD THINGS

New Mexico is full of wildlife. Even in cities such as Santa Fe, bears, mountain lions, and skunks occasionally wander into town. The best way to see animals, though, is to be in the wilds of the state. Elk, deer, porcupines, and bighorn sheep live in the forests. The state's deserts and dry prairies are home to jackrabbits, coyotes, and javelinas, large creatures that look like wild boars and love munching on prickly pear cacti. Rattlesnakes live among the rocks throughout New Mexico. Their bite can be dangerous, but like most animals, they will not bother you if you do not bother them.

Jackrabbits are common in New Mexico's deserts and prairies.

SMOKEY BEAR

Of all the creatures that have ever roamed through New Mexico, none is more famous than Smokey Bear. In 1950 a smoldering cigarette started a devastating forest fire in the south-central part of the state. After firefighters put out the blaze, they discovered a tiny black bear cub hanging on for dear life high up in a scorched pine tree. The creature was badly burned. They named him Smokey.

Although the Forest Service had invented the character Smokey Bear to help prevent forest fires a few years earlier, it wasn't until a real Smokey showed up that the campaign sprang to life. Soon everyone in the country knew about Smokey and the motto, "Only *you* can prevent forest fires." The program was spectacularly successful. Before Smokey, 30 million acres of forest and rangeland burned in the United States each year. By the 1970s that number had dropped to 1 million. Smokey had become so popular and received so much mail that he was given his own zip code.

After Smokey had been discovered and his burns treated, one of his rescuers took him home. The man soon concluded that even baby bears don't make good pets, so Smokey went off to live at the National Zoo in Washington, D.C. After he died, in 1976, he was buried in the village of Capitan, near where he had been found, in what is now the Smokey Bear Historical State Park.

New Mexico also abounds with birds. Hawks soar high overhead, eyeing prey. Finches, thrashers, warblers, and woodpeckers flit among the trees. In the southern half of the state huge black vultures circle slowly over the roads and fields, searching for an easy meal. New Mexico's most famous bird, the roadrunner, grows up to 2 feet long and has a fluffy crest of feathers atop its head. Although roadrunners can fly, they spend most of their time on the ground. It is not unusual to see them racing down the road, sometimes reaching speeds of 20 miles an hour.

New Mexico's state bird is the roadrunner.

The Bosque del Apache National Wildlife Refuge, in the southwestern region, is a paradise for birds and birdwatchers. More than three hundred species of birds can be seen in these wetlands, including herons, egrets, and ducks. Winter is an especially good time to visit because tens of thousands of snow geese, thousands of sandhill cranes, and even a few bald eagles and delicate, endangered whooping cranes come down from colder places in the North.

During the colder months, thousands of snow geese migrate to the Bosque del Apache National Wildlife Refuge.

STATE PARKS

Many parcels of land in New Mexico are protected. The state has five national forests, thirty-four state parks, and many protected wilderness areas and national monuments. Many of the parks are devoted to leisure activities that do not damage the environment, including boating and fishing. The newest protected area is Eagle Nest Lake State Park. The Parks and Monuments department, along with the Game and Fish department, bought the lake from CS Ranch and is now creating facilities so the public can enjoy camping and fishing. The park is located near Wheeler Peak, the highest point in New Mexico, at 13,161 feet.

Although the federal government has attempted to protect wilderness and natural landmarks in New Mexico by declaring areas national forests and parks, at the same time the government has been taking these lands away from the Native Americans. There was a decades-long struggle over Blue Lake, a Taos Pueblo sacred land. President Theodore Roosevelt made it part of Carson National Forest in 1906. The Taos Pueblo reclaimed it in 1970.

HIDDEN COST OF MINING

From 1944 until 1986, 4 million tons of uranium, a precious mineral needed for nuclear weapons and nuclear reactors, was extracted from dozens of mines throughout the Navajo reservation in Arizona, Utah, and New Mexico. This mining operation wrenched uranium from the land using techniques that left behind traces of radioactive material. This material found its way into the land on which animals grazed—animals the Navajo depended on for meat. It contaminated the water that the people and the animals drank. It got into the very bones of the Navajo people living on the reservation. Cancer rates among the Navajo, which had been lower than those of most of the U.S. population, doubled during the period from the early 1970s to the late 1990s.

When the mining companies stopped working the land for uranium ore, they left behind huge piles of tailings, ground-up sand left over after the uranium has been extracted. They also left open pits where water collected. These all continue to threaten the lives of the Navajo who live there. The air still carries radioactive particles, the water still soaks up radioactivity through the ground, and the animals still graze on contaminated grasses.

Today Navajo children still play near a 30-foot-high waste dump, all that is left of the Church Rock Mine; the town of Church Rock was named for this mine. The mine was closed in 1982, but the dump was never cleaned up. The Navajo turned to the Environmental Protection Agency, which administers the Superfund, created to clean up environmental messes like this one.

In 2005 the Navajo Tribal Council banned uranium mining in Navajo country. Now one company hopes to begin mining in Church Rock, New Mexico, in 2008. Three companies have acquired rights to land just outside the reservation boundary and have promised to protect the local water supply. Local residents are skeptical, however. Larry King, a Navajo cattle rancher in Church Rock, says, "All these promises . . . I don't believe a word of it."

PRESERVING THE LAND

In recent years New Mexico has become a battleground between ranchers who want to use the land and environmentalists who want to protect it.

Abandoned mines and their remains are a constant threat to New Mexico's environment.

Overgrazing by cattle is an environmental threat to New Mexico's pastureland.

Much land in New Mexico is owned by the government. Ranchers often lease this public land to graze their cattle. Sometimes cattle are allowed to overgraze, destroying the willow and cottonwood forests along streams and leaving behind barren, crumbling riverbanks. Some birds that nest in these areas have become endangered. Today there are fewer than one thousand breeding pairs of Southwestern willow fly-catchers left. According to Jennifer Fowler-Propst of the U.S. Fish and Wildlife Service, "Their habitat is being lost at an astonishing rate."

Some environmentalists want to halt all grazing on public lands. So much damage has been done, they argue, that ending grazing is the only way to stop these once-green areas from becoming desert. Many ranchers feel picked on. Time and again environmental organizations are "telling people in New Mexico how to run their business," complains Erik Ness of the New Mexico Farm and Livestock Bureau. They argue that they are just trying to make a living, as their parents and grandparents did before them. "This business is ingrained, it's part of you, and somebody comes and takes that away from you. They might as well take your life," says rancher Kit Laney, who has fought hard to continue grazing on public land.

People on both sides of the issue are calling for compromise, although sometimes it's hard to hear them above the din of angry voices. Most ranchers know it is in their economic self-interest to take care of the land. Rick Johnson of the Nature Conservancy says the only way to have healthy stream systems "is for everyone to work together." Only time will tell whether ranchers and environmentalists will find a way to protect the land that they both love.

Chapter Two

A Colorful Past

Although New Mexico was one of the last states admitted to the Union, it has a long and colorful history. Many people do not realize that before the British established their colonies on the East Coast, Spaniards had already built villages in the New Mexican wilderness. And before that—one thousand years ago—Native Americans had constructed fabulous cities there.

THE ANCIENT ONES

Humans have been living in what is now New Mexico for about 12,000 years. In the eastern grasslands ancient peoples pursued giant bison and huge, elephantlike creatures called mammoths that once lived there. As the New Mexican climate became drier, these large mammals died out or headed north, where food was more plentiful.

New Mexico's early inhabitants turned to hunting smaller animals and gathering fruits, nuts, and berries to survive. Over time they began growing corn, squash, and beans. Having a regular supply of food allowed them to build permanent villages. The Mogollon were the first group to settle in one place.

Native Americans were the first to call New Mexico home.

New Mexico's best-known early Native Americans are called the Anasazi, a Navajo word that means "the ancient ones" or "enemy ancestors." Between about C.E. 900 and 1300, the Anasazi constructed great villages out of rocks that they fit together so precisely, the mud mortar they used was often unnecessary. Some Anasazi buildings were five stories high and had hundreds of rooms. The Anasazi sometimes built irrigation systems to water the fields of corn that surrounded their cities. They also made elegant pottery decorated with intricate patterns. Over time the Anasazi developed the most complex civilization north of present-day Mexico.

In New Mexico, ruins are all that remain of the Anasazi culture.

But then something happened. The Anasazi abandoned their cities. No one is sure why, but most likely a severe drought that lasted from 1276 to 1299 forced them off the land. Many headed toward the Rio Grande Valley, where water was more plentiful. They mixed with the Pueblo, who already lived there. The Pueblo lived in houses of rock or adobe, a mixture of earth and straw that has been baked in the sun. In nearby fields they grew corn, squash, and melons.

Around 1500 the Navajo and Apache are thought to have migrated to the Southwest from present-day Canada. The Navajo settled west of the Pueblo, who taught them how to grow corn and beans. The Apache, who spread out over what is now eastern and southern New Mexico, were great hunters and warriors.

THE SPANIARDS ARRIVE

Soon other people wandered into the Southwest. The Spaniards, who had conquered the Native Americans of Mexico in 1521, spent much of their time searching for precious metals. Legend had it that far to the north, beyond great swaths of desolate, unknown land, were the Seven Cities of Cíbola, towns so wealthy that the streets were paved with gold.

In 1539 a party led by Father Marcos de Niza set out in search of the fabled cities. After trudging nearly 2,000 miles, they neared Zuñi Pueblo, in present-day western New Mexico. When one member of the party was killed, Father Marcos left without ever entering the city. He told the Spanish authorities what they wanted to hear: that the Zuñi lived in magnificent villages larger than Mexico City.

The following year Francisco Vásquez de Coronado led an expedition to Zuñi to uncover the riches of Cíbola. When the party arrived there, they found nothing but mud huts. Father Marcos "has not told the truth in a single thing that he has said," Coronado wrote bitterly.

The natives told Coronado that the riches were farther east, most likely to get him to leave. A native guide who led Coronado through the empty plains kept telling him that fabulous cities lay just over the horizon. The expedition traveled as far as present-day Kansas, where they came upon a native Wichita village. Again, there was nothing but huts. Furious at being led on a wild goose chase, Coronado ordered the guide killed. He returned to Mexico City disappointed and disgraced.

Spanish explorer Francisco Vásquez de Coronado trekking on his expedition to Cíbola.

COYOTE BRINGS WINTER: A ZUÑI TALE

This is one of the many Native-American tales featuring the untrustworthy Coyote.

One day, back when the Earth was still new, Eagle and Coyote were out hunting together. They came to the pueblo of the Kachinas, who had a box in which they kept the sun. Whenever the Kachinas wanted light, they opened the box a crack, and the sun peeked out. Then it was day.

"This is wonderful," Coyote said. "Let's steal the box."

"No, that would be wrong," said Eagle. "Let's just borrow it."

When no one was looking, Eagle grabbed the box and flew off. Coyote followed along the ground. He said to Eagle, "Let me carry the box. I am ashamed to let you do all the carrying."

"No, I don't trust you," Eagle answered. "You might open the box and lose this wonderful thing we have borrowed."

Coyote asked again and again, until Eagle finally relented. "You must promise not to open the box," Eagle said.

"I promise," Coyote declared.

When they entered a wooded area, Coyote ducked behind a bush where Eagle could not see him and opened the box. The sun burst out and flew away to the edge of the sky. At once the world grew cold. Leaves fell from the trees, and icy winds blew.

"I should have known better," Eagle said to Coyote. "I should have remembered you never keep a promise. If you had not opened the box, we could have kept the sun near us. We would have had summer all the time. Now we have winter."

Forty years passed before the Spaniards bothered to return to the Rio Grande Valley. Brief forays were made into the region in the 1580s and early 1590s. Then in 1598 Juan de Oñate led a group north to settle New Mexico. They established a village near where the Chama River flows into the Rio Grande and began searching for riches and trying to convert the Native Americans to Christianity.

Not all Pueblo took kindly to being converted. The Acoma lived in a village atop a 357-foot-high mesa. The only way up was by steep, uneven stairs worn into the rock; everywhere else was sheer cliff. The Acoma felt secure in their fortress in the sky. In 1598 a skirmish between the Acoma and Oñate's nephew Juan de Zaldivar left Zaldivar and about a dozen other Spaniards dead. Oñate was outraged. He ordered his men to "burn [Acoma] to the ground, and leave no stone on stone, so that the Native Americans may never be able again to inhabit it." Oñate's men killed eight hundred Native Americans. The Acoma who survived the massacre hardly fared better. Adults were sentenced to twenty years' slavery, and every man over the age of twenty-five not only was enslaved but also had one foot cut off. The Acoma would never forget this horrifying slaughter.

Around 1610 Oñate was called back to Mexico City, where he was tried and convicted of mistreating the Native Americans. That same year the Spanish colonists moved to another

Juan de Oñate established the colony of New Mexico for Spain in 1598.

spot farther south. They called it Santa Fe. Founded just three years after the settlement of Jamestown, Virginia, the first permanent English settlement in the New World, Santa Fe is the oldest capital city in the United States.

THE PUEBLO REVOLT

In the following decades the Spaniards solidified their control over the Rio Grande Valley. They grew crops, raised livestock, and tried to turn the Pueblo into Spaniards. The Spaniards made the Native Americans take on Spanish names and speak only Spanish. They forced them to work in Spanish fields, repair roads, and dig ditches. Worst of all, the Spaniards banned their religion. They prohibited Native-American dances, burned religious objects, and destroyed kivas, the buildings where the Pueblo held sacred ceremonies. Native Americans who continued to practice their religion were whipped, jailed, and sometimes murdered.

Finally the Native Americans rebelled. A medicine man named Popé, who had been imprisoned and whipped, coordinated a revolt among all the Pueblo. On August 10, 1680, Native Americans stormed through the countryside, burning churches and killing priests. "The god of the Spaniards is dead," they shouted, "but our gods will never die." Then they moved toward Santa Fe. For nine days a battle raged. After four hundred Spaniards had been killed, the remaining colonists fled south toward Mexico. For the first and last time Native Americans had driven out their European conquerors.

The Native Americans then tried to erase every shred of evidence that the Spaniards—and their religion—had ever been there. They destroyed Spanish clothing, tools, and animals. They bathed in rivers, trying to scrub off their Christian baptisms. But they could not turn back the clock. After Popé died, the Spaniards easily retook the colony in 1692. The Pueblo would never again be totally independent.

Although the Spaniards were back in control, they had learned from their defeat. They still expected the Native Americans to become at least outwardly Christian, but they no longer destroyed kivas and religious objects. They realized that a more peaceful approach would make life easier for everyone.

THE GROWING COLONY

During the next century the young colony grew slowly, as more settlers traveled north from Mexico. By 1800, ten thousand New Mexicans lived along the northern Rio Grande.

Although technically New Mexico was ruled by officials in Mexico City, those officials were more than 1,000 miles away. The New Mexicans basically governed themselves. Surrounded on all sides by vast, empty lands, New Mexicans knew little of events taking place elsewhere, such as the birth of the United States far away on the East Coast. According to historian Ruth Armstrong, "The American Revolution might have just as well been on another planet for all the difference it made to the Spaniards of New Mexico."

New Mexico's isolation enabled it to develop a unique society. Over the years many Spaniards and Native Americans intermarried and had children. In New Mexico people of mixed ancestry were accepted and could hold important jobs. Many became prominent members of the community, which would have been impossible in Mexico or Spain.

Although a few New Mexicans owned vast ranches, most lived on small farms where they raised just enough crops and livestock to feed themselves. Since Spain didn't allow its colonies to trade with foreign countries, including the United States, any goods that the settlers could not make themselves had to be brought up from Mexico, which took many weeks.

During the nineteenth century New Mexico established settlements in the desert.

In 1821 Mexico declared itself independent from Spain. New Mexico was now part of a new country. The Mexican government immediately decided to allow trade with the United States. That same year a merchant named William Becknell crossed the Great Plains from Missouri with clothing, knives, and other goods. In Santa Fe the New Mexicans eagerly bought all his wares. Becknell made another trip the following year, and the Santa Fe Trail was born. In the coming years many fortunes were made by traders who traveled the harsh 800-mile trail to sell furniture, glassware, candles, and books to the New Mexicans.

Traders traveled the Santa Fe Trail to New Mexico to sell and trade their wares.

BECOMING AMERICAN

The United States and Mexico went to war over a boundary dispute in 1846. That August, American general Stephen Kearney led troops into New Mexico. Facing no resistance from the locals, he climbed to a rooftop in the town of Las Vegas and announced that New Mexico was now part of the United States. This was made official two years later in the Treaty of Guadalupe Hidalgo. From then on Anglos would join Hispanics and Native Americans in building New Mexico's unique society.

There was substantial resistance against the Anglos coming into the territory of New Mexico. Several armed battles took place, including the battles of El Brazito, La Canada, and Embudo Pass, as well as rebellions at Taos and Mora.

In 1862 General James Carleton was sent to New Mexico to subdue the Navajo and Apache, who had been raiding settlers' farms. Carleton minced no words about what he was doing. "There is to be no council held with the Native Americans, nor any talks," he ordered. "The men are to be slain whenever and wherever they can be found. The women and children may be taken prisoners, but, of course, they are not to be killed."

Carleton commanded Colonel Kit Carson to round up the Native Americans and move them onto the Bosque Redondo Reservation on New Mexico's eastern plains. Carson was a complicated man. His wife was from a prominent Hispanic family, and he got along well with New Mexico's Native Americans. He did not like Carleton's policies, but he obeyed orders. When the Navajo refused to move, Carson's men burned their homes, killed their sheep, and destroyed their fields. Facing starvation, the Navajo had little choice but to surrender.

In 1864 thousands of Navajos began trudging 300 miles to Bosque Redondo in what became known as the Long Walk. With little food and inadequate clothing, their journey over snowy mountains and frozen plains turned into a disaster. Hundreds died. The trek was so horrible that to this day, the Navajos date historical events by whether they happened before or after the Long Walk.

Kit Carson was commander of the 1st New Mexico Volunteers.

Conditions on the reservation were no better. Many died of starvation and disease. Eventually U.S. officials had no choice but to admit that their policies had failed and allow the Navajo and Apache to return to reservations in their homelands.

THE WILD WEST

Gradually Americans trickled into what must have seemed a strange and dangerous land. Some planted crops in the fertile valleys. Others sought their fortunes mining silver and gold in the mountains. John Chisum made a fortune, but not from precious metals. Cattle made Chisum rich. In the 1870s he grazed 80,000 cattle on eastern New Mexico's broad plains, which likely made him the biggest cattle rancher in the country.

New Mexico's growing towns were overrun by cowboys, miners, railroad workers, gamblers, and cattle rustlers—but they did not always have sheriffs

New Mexico in the late 1800s attracted cowboys, railroad workers, and gamblers, among others.

to keep the peace. Still an isolated frontier, New Mexico was as wild as any place in the West. Most men wore guns and were more than willing to use them. Emerson Hough, a writer at the time, said New Mexico "was without doubt, as dangerous a country as ever lay out of doors." The northeastern town of Cimarron was particularly notorious. One newspaper reported, "Everything is quiet in Cimarron. Nobody has been killed in three days."

Throughout New Mexico power struggles erupted in violence. In 1878 a feud between rival merchants turned Lincoln County red with blood. The most famous participant in this bloodbath was Billy the Kid. Billy was born in New York City, moved west at age thirteen, and was arrested and escaped from jail for the first time at fifteen. His charm and explosive temper were legendary. According to Sheriff Pat Garrett, who eventually killed him, the Kid's "face always wore a smile. He ate and laughed, drank and laughed, rode and laughed, talked and laughed, fought and laughed— and killed and laughed."

The Kid was convicted of murdering the Lincoln County sheriff, but before he could be hanged, he escaped, killing two deputies on the way out. When Garrett gunned him down two months later, Billy the Kid was twenty-one years old.

Billy the Kid earned himself the reputation of being a cold-blooded killer.

BILLY THE KID

Henry McCarty, also known as William H. Bonney, who came to be known as Billy the Kid, was born in New York City on November 23, 1859. His family moved west, and he eventually found himself in Silver City, New Mexico. Over the years his reputation as a cold-blooded killer grew and grew until he was shot to death by his former friend Sheriff Pat Garrett on July 14, 1881. Then legend took over and portrayed him as a folk hero.

go, Where a man's on-ly friend was his old for-ty four.

When Billy the Kid was a very young lad,
In old Silver City he went to the bad.
Way out in the West with a gun in his hand,
At the age of twelve years he killed his first man.

Young Mexican maidens play guitars and sing
Songs about Billy, their boy bandit king,
How there's a young man who had reached his sad end—
Had a notch on his pistol for twenty-one men.

It was on the same night when poor Billy died,
He said to his friends, "I'm not satisfied.
There are twenty-one men I have put bullets through—
Sheriff Pat Garrett must make twenty-two."

Now this is how Billy the Kid met his fate,
The bright moon was shining the hour was late.
Shot down by Pat Garrett who once was his friend,
The young outlaw's life had now reached its sad end.

Now there's many a lad with a face fine and fair,
Who starts out in life with a chance to be square,
But just like poor Billy they wander astray,
They lose their life in the very same way.

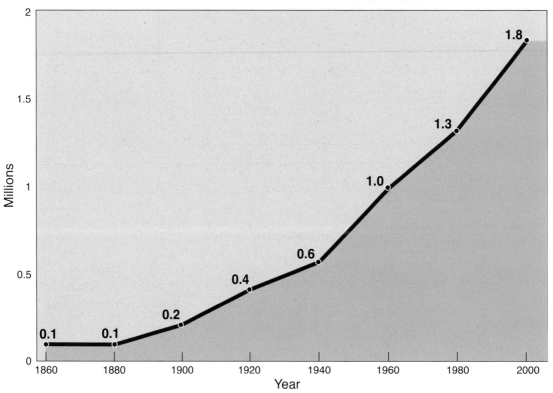

POPULATION GROWTH: 1860–2000

Millions (y-axis): 2, 1.5, 1, 0.5, 0

Year (x-axis): 1860, 1880, 1900, 1920, 1940, 1960, 1980, 2000

Data points: 0.1, 0.1, 0.2, 0.4, 0.6, 1.0, 1.3, 1.8

THE LONG ROAD TO STATEHOOD

New Mexico's reputation for lawless chaos often prompted people to repeat General William Tecumseh Sherman's joke that "The United States ought to declare war on Mexico and make it take back New Mexico." From the time New Mexico became a U.S. territory, politicians in Washington had railed against granting political equality to New Mexicans, the majority of whom were Hispanic. "Ours, sir, is the government of a white race," roared Senator John C. Calhoun of South Carolina. As the years passed, many people remained suspicious of New Mexico, where people spoke a different language and enjoyed different customs.

They argued that New Mexicans could never be true Americans. Again and again New Mexico was denied statehood.

Only with the Spanish-American War, in 1898, when the United States helped the island nation of Cuba throw off Spanish rule, did these attitudes finally change. Some people had questioned whether New Mexicans, many of whom were of Spanish descent, would be loyal to the United States. The New Mexicans answered them loud and clear. Half of Theodore Roosevelt's famous Rough Riders regiment were New Mexicans. By the war's end they had proven themselves so loyal, so brave, that no one could doubt their commitment to America. Finally, in 1912, after sixty-two years as a territory, New Mexico became the forty-seventh state.

Theodore Roosevelt and his Rough Riders on San Juan Hill in Cuba.

"VIVA VILLA!"

In the early hours of the morning of March 9, 1916, a band of Mexican revolutionaries led by the famed general and bandit Pancho Villa crept over the border into the town of Columbus, New Mexico. For years Mexico had been in chaos, with various factions vying for power. President Woodrow Wilson had recognized one of Villa's enemies, Venustiano Carranza, as the official leader of Mexico. Villa was angry.

The rebels wreaked havoc on Columbus. Amid shouts of *"Viva Villa, viva Mexico!"* ("Long live Villa, long live Mexico!"), they burned houses, shot citizens, and collected whatever guns, ammunition, and other supplies they could find. After members of the U.S. Cavalry stationed nearby awoke, the battle was on. By the time dawn broke, the Mexicans had retreated south, and Columbus was in smoldering ruins. Eighteen Americans and about ninety Mexicans had been killed. It was the first and only time in the twentieth century that a foreign force invaded the United States.

President Wilson sent General John Pershing and more than six thousand soldiers into Mexico to capture Villa, but they were no match for the harsh Mexican terrain. After chasing Villa for almost a year, Pershing returned home empty-handed, ending the strange saga of the sacking of Columbus.

As the century progressed, more and more people found reason to venture to New Mexico. Some came because their doctors told them the clear air would cure tuberculosis, a deadly disease that often affects the lungs. Painters, photographers, and writers were drawn by the state's blinding beauty. The military discovered that New Mexico's uncluttered plains were ideal for air force bases.

TO THE PRESENT

In 1943 a group of newcomers took over the Los Alamos Ranch School in the Jemez Mountains. Hundreds of people who got off the train in Santa Fe and were whisked to the remote site did not even know where they were being taken. Each was given a driver's license with a number instead of a name. Their project was so secret that only people who could not read were hired to empty their garbage cans.

They had been brought together to develop the atomic bomb, the most destructive weapon the world had ever known. The United States was in the midst of World War II and believed it had to make the bomb before its enemies did.

On July 16, 1945, the secret of what all those people were doing in the mountains was revealed. In the desert of south-central New Mexico the world's first atomic bomb was detonated. The blinding orange flash was visible in Santa Fe, nearly 150 miles away. At the blast site temperatures as hot as that of the sun caused the sand to melt into glass. In a nearby bunker Robert J. Oppenheimer, the project's leader, muttered an ancient Hindu quotation: "I am become Death, destroyer of the worlds." Within a month atomic bombs had leveled the Japanese cities of Hiroshima and Nagasaki. World War II was over, but the world had changed. The atomic age had arrived.

On July 16, 1945, the world's first atomic bomb was detonated in Alamogordo, New Mexico.

NAVAJO CODE TALKERS

During World War II the Navajo people contributed greatly to the American war effort in a very unique way. The U.S. Marine Corps used Navajo soldiers as "code talkers." During the war with Japan, enemy code breakers were able to crack almost every kind of encoded communication, but they weren't able to crack the "code" of the Navajo language. Units that needed to communicate without having the enemy understand the messages being sent would use Navajo soldiers to transmit their messages in the Navajo language. These soldiers could transmit information in minutes. Major Howard Connor, who served in World War II, supervised six Navajo code talkers. He said, "Were it not for the Navajos, the Marines would never have taken Iwo Jima." During the war 540 Navajos served as Marines; about 400 of them were trained as code talkers. Because of the secrecy of their mission, their important role in the war was not recognized until 2001, when they were awarded the Congressional Medal of Honor.

In 2006, five of the surviving code talkers came to Albuquerque to take part in the Gathering of Nations Powwow. These men were recognized by everyone for the tremendous role they played during the war.

New Mexico profited greatly from the atomic age, as military bases and research laboratories multiplied within its borders. The state's growing economy and warm, dry climate attracted throngs of newcomers. By the 1950s Albuquerque, the state's largest city, was bursting at the seams. "New houses go up in batches of fifty to three hundred at a time, and transform the barren mesas before you get back from lunch," one journalist commented.

TENSIONS STILL SIMMER

There is still racial tension to be found in New Mexico, and it can sometimes find its way to the surface. On June 4, 2006, three white men beat a Navajo man, William Blackie, and shouted racial slurs at him. That same week another Navajo, Clint John, was killed by a white police officer. These incidents brought out one thousand Navajo residents, who marched to protest and to remember incidents from the 1970s. In 1975 racial prejudice against Native Americans in the town of Farmington was considered so widespread, it generated an investigation by the U.S. Commission on Civil Rights. While the current incidents stand out because they are so much rarer, others say that attitudes toward Native Americans have not changed very much. "The bias, the unfairness, this has been going on all along," according to Larry Emerson, chairman of the New Mexico Indian Education Advisory Council. Many crimes against Navajos go unreported, he added.

Sadly, New Mexico has also been caught up in a cultural battle that is going to change the face of United States–Mexican relations. Toward the end of 2006 the U. S. government took a dramatic step to try to stem the tide of illegal emigration from Mexico into the United States. It announced a plan to build a 700-mile-long fence along the 2,000-mile-long border between the two nations. The first sections of the wall to be built include a stretch along the New Mexico–Mexico border from the point where New Mexico touches Texas, westward to Columbus, where Pancho Villa famously crossed over from Mexico in 1916. But the local people say this is just foolish. "That stretch is one of the most rugged parts of the country," said a man running a photo-processing shop in Albuquerque. "That's not where people cross over from Mexico."

As for the bill proposed by the House of Representatives that would make it a crime to stay in the United States without legal documentation, Alicia Salazar, a high school sophomore, says, "You're not a felon if you want a better life for your family."

Border-patrol workers erect a fence along the New Mexico–Mexico border. This portion will be 1.3 miles long and 10 feet tall upon completion.

Chapter Three

Proud Traditions

Several different ethnic groups, each with its own proud history and traditions, have contributed to New Mexico's distinct character. Until recently non-Hispanics were in the majority, but just barely. By 2005 the figures showed that the two main ethnic groups were nearly equal in numbers. New Mexicans of Hispanic descent made up 43.4 percent of the population, just edging out the Anglos, who made up 43.1 percent of the population. This percentage of the population of Hispanic origin is the highest of any state in the Union. New Mexico also has the greatest percentage of Native Americans among the states—about 10 percent of the population. The state has a growing number of African Americans and Asians as well. Over the centuries these groups have created a multicultural state in the truest sense. Each group has its own traditions and history.

THREE CULTURES

New Mexico's Native Americans have had more success maintaining their languages, religions, and traditions than Native Americans in

A dancer from the Baile Español performs at El Rancho de las Golondrinas, a living history ranch that celebrates the Native-American and Hispanic cultures of Sante Fe.

most other parts of the United States. Today young Native Americans may work in the laboratories of Los Alamos and then return to their villages to participate in ceremonies during feast days.

Some New Mexican Native Americans continue to make the handicrafts passed down from their parents and grandparents. The Navajo are renowned for their beautiful woven rugs and turquoise jewelry. Apache baskets are prized.

Duane Maktima is a Native American of mixed Laguna Pueblo and Hopi heritage who makes award-winning jewelry. He draws on Native-American traditions along with contemporary silversmithing techniques to create intricate and beautiful jewelry. He treasures turquoise, considered the most important and precious stone by Native Americans, and often uses it in his designs. His studio is in a rural area a few miles outside Santa Fe. From there he can walk in the mountains and forests of Pecos Wilderness and find the peace and tranquility he needs to design. His work is greatly influenced by the time he spent living with his extended family at Laguna Pueblo in New Mexico. He sees his work as an integral part of his Native-American ancestry. "My grandfather always said that from sunup to sundown, you should be doing something of value, and now I feel that I am."

A Navajo father teaches his son the art of jewelry making.

The Pueblo are famous for their pottery. Each village has its own style of pottery. Some use many colors; others use only black and white. While some craftspeople decorate their pots with geometric designs, others look to nature for inspiration. For many Native Americans creating pottery is more than a way to make a living. It is a vital part of their culture and a connection to the past. When Acoma are born, they are bathed in a pottery bowl. When they die, they are buried with pottery. "We come into this world with pottery and we are going to leave the earth with pottery," says Acoma potter Dolores Garcia.

Pottery is a central part of the Acoma's traditions and heritage.

PUEBLO FEAST DAYS

The Pueblo sometimes allow outsiders to visit during feast days. This is a great way to learn about their culture.

Often the celebrations mix aspects of the traditional Pueblo religion with Christianity. On Christmas Eve at San Felipe Pueblo, the spirits of the animal kingdom come to honor the baby Jesus. In this striking ritual, deer dancers wearing antler headdresses step softly, while buffalo dancers wearing horned headdresses and fur stamp thunderously.

San Geronimo Day at Taos Pueblo features dancing and a trade fair, which includes displays of drums, pottery, and beaded moccasins. Young men participate in footraces. Black-and-white–striped clowns wearing corn husks in their hair climb a greased pole to reach bundles of food at the top and tease the people in the crowd. All in all, it is one of the most lighthearted Pueblo feast days.

New Mexico's Hispanics are proud of their long history in the region. They point out that their families were granted land in New Mexico by the Spanish crown long before the United States even existed. Today some New Mexicans worry that the younger generations are forgetting their heritage. "Children today do not speak Spanish—in my grandmother's house, we were not allowed to speak English," says Frank Ortiz, whose family has been living in northern New Mexico since 1607. Although New Mexico's Hispanics have adapted to many changes over the centuries, their pride in their heritage is unwavering.

New Mexico's Hispanic population retains its culture by maintaining Old World traditions.

New Mexico's Anglos also have a colorful heritage to draw upon. It took courage and self-reliance for miners and cowboys to venture into this harsh, remote land. Their sons and daughters often exhibit a similar independent streak. "They can't make me wear a seatbelt, can't make me use matches that you strike on the box, and can't make me use a computer. I'm an old woman," says one seventy-year-old. Today New Mexicans recall their frontier history in events such as Fort Sumner's Old Fort Days, which features a rodeo and a staged bank robbery.

ETHNIC NEW MEXICO

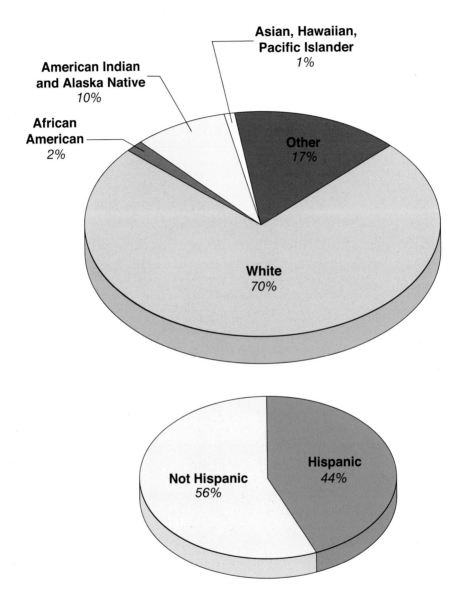

Asian, Hawaiian, Pacific Islander
1%

American Indian and Alaska Native
10%

African American
2%

Other
17%

White
70%

Not Hispanic
56%

Hispanic
44%

Note: A person of Cuban, Mexican, Puerto Rican, South or Central American, or other Spanish culture or origin, regardless of race, is defined as Hispanic.

SEARCHING FOR PARADISE

In recent decades newcomers have swarmed into towns across New Mexico. Some are retired folks attracted by the state's pleasant climate and invigorating air. Others are wealthy Californians searching for a weekend getaway. Artists and others are looking for a beautiful place where the cost of living is low. New Mexico's ridges, valleys, and rocky deserts make ideal refuges for people who want to escape city life, who want to be closer to nature and live in a simpler way. They also appeal to anyone who just wants to be left alone.

The influx of newcomers has changed many New Mexico towns. "Between when this town was founded in 1877 and 1995 the only place around here you could get wet was in the creek down there.

New Mexico has become a popular destination, drawing many with its climate, beauty, and culture.

Now there's three houses with swimming pools," says one Hillsboro resident. No matter why they come, the recent arrivals drive up land prices, often putting homes out of the reach of longtime residents of New Mexico, which is among the poorest states in the nation.

Nowhere is this more true than in Santa Fe. Its dusty streets and adobe architecture have long charmed visitors, inspiring them to stay. Adobe houses are made of sun-dried bricks of earth and straw. Rough beams called vigas, which hold up the flat roof, stick all the way through the walls to the outside. Many people love adobe's warm feel and the way its brown, curved shapes blend so easily into the landscape.

Although adobe architecture is found all over New Mexico, it is most closely associated with Santa Fe. Practically every building in Santa Fe is some shade of brown. But these days, only the rich can afford real adobe homes. Many other houses that look like adobe are actually ordinary houses covered with stucco and painted brown. Often they have the corner fireplaces typical of real adobe houses. Some even have imitation vigas. Some people complain that Santa Fe has become a southwestern theme park. They call the town "Santa Fake."

In 1990, for the first time, Hispanics made up less than half the city's population. "The white people moved in, painted the town brown and moved the brown people out," says former mayor Debbie Jaramillo. Priced out of their hometown, some Santa Feans have moved to Albuquerque, a more affordable city with better job opportunities. But many others love their town too much to abandon it.

CELEBRATING TOGETHER

Every September the people of Santa Fe hold the Fiesta de Santa Fe to commemorate the Spaniards' return to the city after the Pueblo Revolt.

The first fiesta was celebrated in 1712—no other community celebration in the United States dates back that far. During the fiesta, Santa Fe overflows with street dances, concerts, and processions. Parades featuring floats, low-rider cars, and children and their pets dressed in costumes bring life and color to the city streets.

Christmas is a magical time in New Mexico. All over the state people line streets, walls, and rooftops with small paper bags containing glowing candles propped in sand. These decorations, called *farolitos* in northern New Mexico and luminaries in Albuquerque and farther south, create a lovely wavering orange light. In Santa Fe tens of thousands of people step out into the chilly night air on Christmas Eve. They stroll around town, enjoying the flickering displays, sipping hot cider, and perhaps marveling at how lucky they are to live in a place that is truly enchanting.

Luminaries light up Santa Fe during the holidays.

ALBUQUERQUE CELEBRATES

In April 2006 the Hispanic community celebrated the three-hundredth anniversary of the founding of Albuquerque. It was a colorful and festive day, with descendants of the original conquistadores riding into Old Town, the historic center, on horseback. Men, women, and children wore traditional clothes as they paraded through the adobe-lined streets. Some had ridden for 28 miles along the Rio Grande, south from Bernalillo to Albuquerque. In the central plaza of Old Town they reenacted the granting of the land given to the Spanish newcomers. Presiding over the ceremony was Mayor Martin Chavez, who was dressed in traditional clothes and portraying the city's first mayor, Capitan Martin Hurtado, handing out land deeds and greeting

Descendants of the families who founded Albuquerque carry banners displaying their families' coats of arms.

descendants of the original families. One participant, Samuel Ulibarri, is a thirteenth-generation descendant of Capitan Juan de Ulibarri, whom he portrayed during the ceremony. On hand on this day were the duke and duchess of Alburquerque (the original spelling), who had traveled from Spain to the city named for their family. The name was chosen by the colonial governor, Don Francisco Cuervo y Valdez.

This was a time for outsiders to consider the impact these new arrivals had on the existing Native-American peoples who lived on these lands. They were not part of this ceremony, which celebrated the loss of those lands to the well-armed Spanish. This site, on the banks of the Rio Grande, was chosen specifically because the newcomers found the region "pleasant, well watered and of a healthy climate."

Those qualities were well known to the Native Americans, who had been living throughout the region for at least a thousand years. Their careful stewardship of the land and their understanding of the plants, the seasons, and the natural resources made it possible for them to survive in a physical environment that was very demanding. But the arrival of the Spanish meant the beginning of the loss of their lands and the dismissal of the value of their cultures.

The day after the three-hundredth anniversary celebrations the Native Americans began their own celebration. It was the start of the Gathering of Nations Powwow. This was a rare privilege and unique opportunity for visitors to join in the celebration. More than three thousand dancers and singers from five hundred Indian tribes, or nations, came together to dance at an arena called "The Pit," part of the University of New Mexico. Dancing is an expression of the native peoples' culture, and the sights and sounds they presented transported the visitors out of the modern arena. Drummers were placed in groups around the floor and kept the beat for the dancers.

Dancers participate at the Gathering of Nations Powwow.

Next came the women jingle dancers, named for their ornament-covered skirts that make a jingly sound as they dance. There was a healing song from the Montana women. There was a tremendous display of women "dancing their style," each one showing off her unique footwork as she danced around the floor with a solemn face. As more and more women joined in, the entire floor was filled with dancers, all moving as one and yet individually. These were followed by the "golden age women," the dancers up to the age of seventy. The group older than that is called "the elders." Each group made the same movements, but at different speeds. Even the oldest dancers showed the grace and style of the younger ones. The continuity of the generations could be seen on that dance floor.

Between dance exhibitions New Mexico's Archbishop Sheehan spoke: "We thank you for your love of the land and for keeping the land clean and pure and for your ancestors and we pray and bless you. We love you for your spiritual traditions. The Native Americans came to teach us spiritual truths we could never know on our own."

ZOZOBRA

"Burn him, burn him," chant 40,000 Santa Feans one Friday evening. The object of their ill will is a 40-foot-tall wood and papier-mâché monster named Zozobra, also known as Old Man Gloom. Since 1926 Santa Feans have washed away their troubles and misfortunes by burning Zozobra.

As a fire dancer with a blazing torch circles the huge white puppet, the monster moans and groans, thrashes his arms, and bobs his head, trying to scare the dancer off. But the fire dancer always wins, and the crowd gives a great cheer as Zozobra begins to burn. The monster's eyes turn glowing red, and flames pour from his mouth. In three minutes he is gone. Nothing remains but a wire framework and ashes wafting over the crowd.

With that, all the gloom of the previous year has been wiped away, and the Fiesta de Santa Fe is off and running.

POPULATION DENSITY

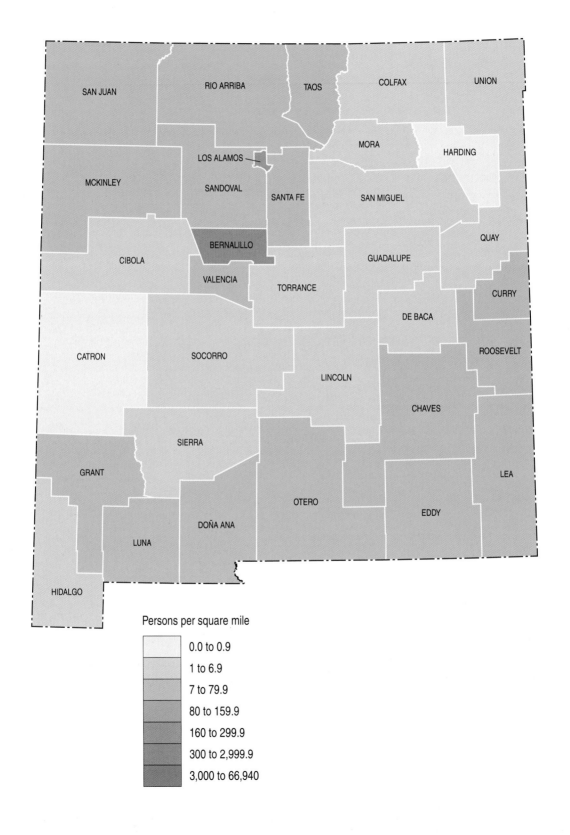

Persons per square mile

- 0.0 to 0.9
- 1 to 6.9
- 7 to 79.9
- 80 to 159.9
- 160 to 299.9
- 300 to 2,999.9
- 3,000 to 66,940

VILLAGE LIFE

New Mexico is sprinkled with small towns and villages where the residents have deep roots and loyalties. In Las Trampas, a village between Santa Fe and Taos that is so small it doesn't even get a dot on many maps, most people are content to remain where their families have lived for hundreds of years. Just eighty people live in the town, but the population is not dropping, and very few outside families have moved in. Although some people go away to college or off to work elsewhere for a while, most eventually return, drawn home by the crisp air and the beautiful mountain scenery. "Everybody comes back," said Leroy Aguilar, whose family has lived in Las Trampas since the 1760s.

Although these tiny towns provide peace and a sense of community, living in them can be a challenge. Hillsboro, for instance, has no school, so children have to ride the bus more than 30 miles to the nearest town with a school. Hillsboro does not have many job opportunities, either. Nor do these villages have the conveniences that most people expect.

According to a shopkeeper in Las Trampas, "When you get old and sick, you have to move to Santa Fe because there's no medical services here. So then you have to leave, when you need to go to the doctor regularly."

Still, the man concludes, "Other than that, it's perfect. You gave me a million dollars, I wouldn't move away from here. It's my village. I belong here."

The Sierra Blanca rise 12,000 feet above the mountain village of Ruidoso.

Chapter Four

Growing and Changing

New Mexico's government is organized according to its state constitution, which was adopted in 1911. Most sections of the constitution can be changed if a majority of voters agrees. But out of respect for the state's unique history, changing sections that protect the voting rights and education of Spanish-speaking people requires a greater percentage. Two-thirds of the voters in each county and three-quarters of the voters as a whole must agree.

INSIDE GOVERNMENT

Like the federal government and the governments of other states, New Mexico's government has three divisions: executive, legislative, and judicial.

Executive

The head of New Mexico's executive branch is the governor, who is elected to a four-year term. Before a bill passed by the legislature becomes law, the governor must sign it. He or she also appoints many important state officials, such as some members of the board of finance.

New Mexico's state capitol is built in the Pueblo Indian adobe style, in the shape of the Zia Indian sun symbol.

New Mexico's legislature is made up of forty-two senators, who are elected to four-year terms, and seventy representatives, who are elected to two-year terms. The legislature proposes and votes on bills. If a majority of both the senate and the house of representatives votes for a bill and the governor signs it, it becomes law. If the governor vetoes, or rejects, the bill, it can still become law if enough legislators vote to override the veto.

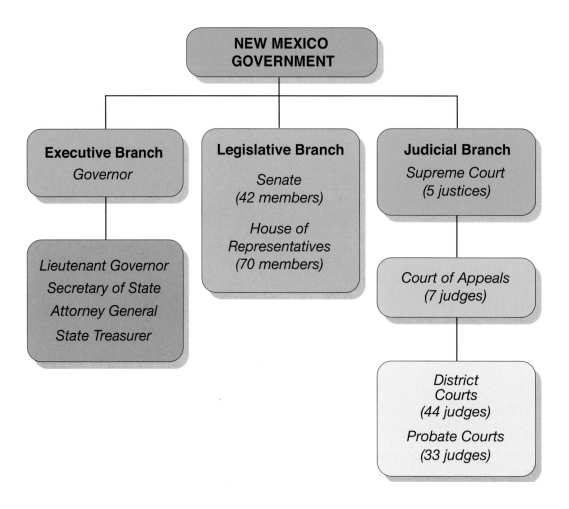

NEW MEXICO GOVERNMENT

Executive Branch
Governor

Lieutenant Governor
Secretary of State
Attorney General
State Treasurer

Legislative Branch
Senate
(42 members)

House of Representatives
(70 members)

Judicial Branch
Supreme Court
(5 justices)

Court of Appeals
(7 judges)

District Courts
(44 judges)

Probate Courts
(33 judges)

Judicial

New Mexico's highest court is the supreme court, which has five justices who are elected to eight-year terms. The supreme court determines whether laws enacted by the legislature violate the state constitution. The justices also decide whether cases decided in lower courts were handled properly. The state's primary trial courts are called district courts. If someone disagrees with a decision made in a district court, he or she can ask the court of appeals to review it. Most cases heard by the court of appeals can also be appealed to the supreme court.

Changes to the constitution continue to be made in the twenty-first century. Among them were decisions in 2003 to create a cabinet-level public education department, a permanent fund for land-grant distributions, and several changes aimed at lifting the burden of property taxes on veterans.

HISPANIC TUESDAY

The importance of the Hispanic vote in New Mexico was recognized when the state played host to a Democratic Party caucus. A caucus is a meeting where candidates come together to present their ideas and try to line up backers who will nominate them to run for political office. In 2004 New Mexico was one of seven states holding their caucuses in February. Both New Mexico and neighboring Arizona have large Hispanic populations, and this led political analysts to dub these primaries as "Hispanic Tuesday."

Governor Bill Richardson was very enthusiastic about the attention this brought to the state, saying, "New Mexicans will now have a say in who will be the next Democratic candidate for president of the United States." Events such as this highlight the issues that are important to the state, issues with which some candidates are not familiar.

Bilingual voting signs encourage voters to cast their ballots.

"Hispanic and Native American issues are now included," Richardson added. "In addition, the issues important to New Mexico and other western states—water, energy, jobs and the environment—are getting the attention they deserve." Shining a spotlight on New Mexico to bring these issues to the attention of the entire nation is not an easy task, since the state has such a small population—fewer than two million people. Since Richardson has name recognition outside the state, he is able to bring the state's special needs to a wider audience.

NEW LEADERSHIP

New Mexico's dynamic governor, Bill Richardson, was first elected in 2003 and then reelected for a second term in 2006. In many ways he has put New Mexico into the national spotlight. Not only is he an engaging and enthusiastic promoter of his state, but he has national recognition, a factor that led Richardson to declare himself a candidate for the presidential election in 2008.

At his inauguration as governor Richardson said, "Being re-elected governor of the state I love is the greatest honor I've ever had."

According to Trip Jennings, writer for the *Albuquerque Journal* newspaper, in Richardson's first term, "He consolidated power, toughened the state's DWI [driving while under the influence of alcohol] laws, cut taxes, boosted the film industry . . . took steps to budge the state's lagging public schools forward . . ."

With a Mexican mother, Richardson has a personal connection to immigration and border issues. He supports a Senate bill that would lead the nation's millions of illegal immigrants to permanent and legal residence. At the same time he is working to get government funds to help control the flow of illegal drugs into the country along the southern border. "As Border Governors," he says, "we are on the front lines of the fight against drug smugglers and other illegal activity."

Richardson has also played a role on the world stage. Using his experience as a former ambassador to the United Nations, Richardson traveled to the war-torn Darfur region of Sudan.

New Mexico's governor Bill Richardson is dedicated to the growth and strength of the state.

He went there to persuade the warring factions to agree to a cease-fire, hoping that would lead to an end to the terrible violence that has killed more than 200,000 people.

NATIVE-AMERICAN AFFAIRS

In 2006 the Bureau of Indian Affairs inaugurated the Manuel Lujan Jr. Indian Affairs Building in Albuquerque. The building houses the Department of the Interior's National Indian Programs Training Center. The training center offers courses for some 15,000 people a year, and the building consolidates all of the Bureau of Indian Affairs (BIA) employees in Albuquerque. The opening of the building was a joyous and spectacular event, with dancers from several Indian tribes performing. The building was named for the former secretary of the interior who served under President George H. W. Bush. In addition to housing the BIA, the building houses the federal employees who deal with various aspects of Native-American life, including the Office of the Special Trustee, the Bureau of Land Management, and the office of the Minerals Management Service.

Native-American land issues are extremely complicated. Through the centuries, as populations grew, the land held by Native Americans was divided over and over again. Eventually people who inherited land found it too small a piece to be useful. Some of the parcels of land had a value of less than a dollar, yet the U.S. Government's Bureau of Indian Affairs had an obligation to keep track of each and every bit of it. The paperwork required to do this cost as much as forty dollars a year to complete for each bit of land. Now, through the Indian Land Consolidation Project, a plan has been put into effect to solve this problem. New Mexico resident Scott Sucher, a retired twenty-year veteran of the U.S. Air Force, has been put in charge of traveling all over the country, buying up bits of land. He acts as a middleman between all the tribes' members, putting together these pieces of land and creating larger, more useful tracts. "Once I get the land together," Sucher says, "the tribe gets it back and can derive economic benefit from it. No one benefits from the little pieces. And, the American taxpayer wins because the government doesn't have to keep track of it anymore."

A Jicarilla Apache on the tribe's reservation in New Mexico.

NEW MEXICO BY COUNTY

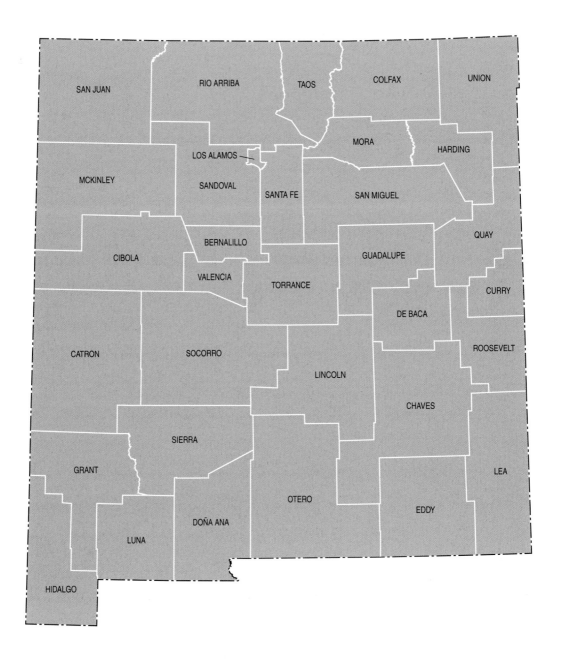

GROWING CITIES

As New Mexico's sunshine and clean air draw more and more people to its cities, the problems these cities face grow and change. In the last few years muggings, robbery, and vandalism have become increasingly common in Santa Fe. Some people think this is inevitable. "Crime is a problem partly because the population is growing," says city councilor Cris Moore.

Albuquerque faces its own problems. As its population has grown, the city has spread into the surrounding hills and plains, replacing piñon trees and cacti with housing developments and strip malls. This sprawl strains the government, which must build roads and provide services to ever more distant communities. And since more and more commuters drive farther and farther to work each day, the developments contribute to air pollution. "We now understand as a community that if we continue to sprawl, we won't be able to either service the new areas or improve our air quality," says one local official.

To try to slow the sprawl, the city is encouraging developers to build in empty sites within the city rather than in previously undeveloped areas. Albuquerque is also trying to persuade stores and businesses to locate near homes, so people can walk where they want to go, rather than always having to get in the car. With government and business working together, the people of New Mexico hope that Albuquerque will continue to grow and prosper without polluting the air that draws people to it.

A housing development encroaches upon Petroglyph National Monument in Albuquerque.

Chapter Five

Making a Living

In his 2007 State of the State address, Governor Bill Richardson said, "Today, our economy is strong and growing stronger. We created more than 80,000 jobs during the past four years. Our unemployment rate plummeted from 5.8 percent to 4.3 percent. And average income is growing—tenth fastest in the nation." Half of the new jobs came from construction and the government. The government will continue to be the greatest contributor of new jobs to the state. Over the five-year period between 2005 and 2010, more than 20,000 new government jobs will be created.

To help New Mexicans, Richardson proposed an increase of the minimum wage, to $7.50 an hour. "We should not wait for Washington," he said. "We must do what's right for the working men and women who drive our economy." He also proposed eliminating the state income tax for members of the U.S. military on active duty.

The U.S. government is a major employer in New Mexico. For decades the military has been taking advantage of the state's flat, dry expanses to build air force bases and testing fields. Los Alamos National Laboratories and Sandia National Laboratories, which is Albuquerque's largest employer, are among the world's leaders in scientific research.

A New Mexico resident hangs a string of chilies to dry.

SPACEPORT

The newest addition to the state's scientific ventures is Spaceport America, near Upham, New Mexico. Plans are underway to have it operating by late 2009 or early 2010. The site, a remote location that offers open airspace, few people, and a high elevation, is considered ideal for rocket launches. The project has attracted attention from aerospace companies as well as from Richard Branson, owner of the Virgin companies. He plans to establish the world headquarters of his Virgin Galactic "spaceline" in New Mexico. Creation of the spaceport has already generated much road building. The spaceport is intended, some day, to be the launching pad for sending tourists into space. Although most of the construction is still in the future, the spaceport is expected to generate nearly 5,800 jobs. Before any of that happens, however, New Mexico must come up with a huge investment of $225 million just to get the project going.

TOURISM AND MOVIES

Tourism is also vital to the New Mexican economy. More than 12 million people visit the state each year to enjoy its ski slopes, cafés, pueblos, and caves. They allow motel owners, shopkeepers, craftspeople, and cooks to earn a living. But sometimes the people who live off tourism resent these outsiders for coming in and taking over their towns, clogging their streets, and driving up prices. "A lot of people don't like the tourism, but at the same time, there's nothing else," says Andrea Lopez, who runs a fajita stand in Santa Fe. Still, she sees tourism as preferable to industry, which might harm the environment. Although little manufacturing takes place in Santa Fe, elsewhere in the state, New Mexicans make computer chips, telephone equipment, scientific instruments, appliances, and printed materials.

Tourists shop for jewelry on the Plaza in Sante Fe.

New Mexico's amazing landscape was the setting for two major films that brought tremendous investment to the state. *Once Upon a Time in the Hood*, a movie starring Steven Seagal, was filmed in and around Albuquerque at the end of 2006 and provided jobs for dozens of locals as members of the crew. Another, *Tennessee*, with Mariah Carey, was shot in 2007 and provided jobs for about fifty New Mexicans as crew members. According to the New Mexico Department of Labor, more than fifty feature films and television shows were shot in the state during the four years of Governor Richardson's first term in office, contributing more than $850 million to the state's economy.

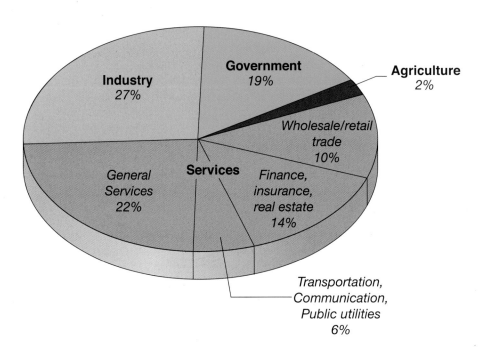

2005 GROSS STATE PRODUCT: $69 Billion

- Industry 27%
- Government 19%
- Agriculture 2%
- Wholesale/retail trade 10%
- General Services 22%
- Services
- Finance, insurance, real estate 14%
- Transportation, Communication, Public utilities 6%

AGRICULTURE

Many ranchers graze cattle and sheep on the sparse vegetation that grows on New Mexico's plains because the dry, rocky soil makes farming difficult. In the eastern part of the state irrigation has enabled farmers to grow hay, wheat, and cotton. Along the Rio Grande pecans and chiles are leading crops. The town of Hatch is a center for chile production. In late summer and early fall the main road through Hatch is lined with farmstands selling the freshest and tastiest chiles around.

Farming is a hard way to make a living. Between late freezes that destroy crops and falling prices that eliminate profits, uncertainty is the norm. "Sometimes, I get so disgusted and depressed that I feel like quitting," says Orlando Casados Jr., a chile farmer near the town of Española. "But come spring, you just feel like getting out there on the tractor and doing it all over again. Chile is our heritage. I just think that somewhere along the line, if we keep up the tradition, it will pay off." His father, Orlando Sr., who started the farm, agrees that working the land is worth the headaches. "Farming is a nice little life," he says. "You never get rich, but it's a nice little life."

Chilies are a major crop in New Mexico.

SALSA

Chile peppers give New Mexico's spicy food its fire. Some kinds of chilies are much hotter than others. The Scoville Heat Scale tells how much burn a chile has. Bell peppers have no fire and barely register on the scale. Jalapeños score five thousand. But that's nothing compared to habañeros, which soar to between 200,000 and 300,000 Scoville units.

Chilies are an important ingredient in salsa, a delicious concoction New Mexicans cannot get enough of. They put it on everything—eggs, tacos, hamburgers. Of course, it's good with tortilla chips, too.

Choose your chile based on how hot you like your food. Have an adult help you with this recipe.

2 medium tomatoes
1 medium onion
1 clove garlic
1/2 teaspoon salt
2 green chilies

Wear rubber gloves when handling chilies, and do not touch your eyes! Peel the chilies and remove their seeds. Chop the chilies, tomatoes, and onions finely. Crush the garlic and blend it with the salt. Mix everything together. Let sit for about an hour so the flavors can mingle. Enjoy—on anything!

The first Spaniards who came to New Mexico were searching for gold and silver. Although they didn't find any, vast riches were hidden beneath the earth. New Mexico is among the leading states in the production of natural gas, oil, and potash, which is used in making fertilizer. New Mexico also has more copper in the ground than almost any other state. Some 300 million pounds of copper are removed each year from the Santa Rita Copper Mine, one of the oldest operating mines in North America. Today it is a mile-wide canyon, and the town of Santa Rita that used to sit atop it is long gone.

NEW MEXICO WORKFORCE

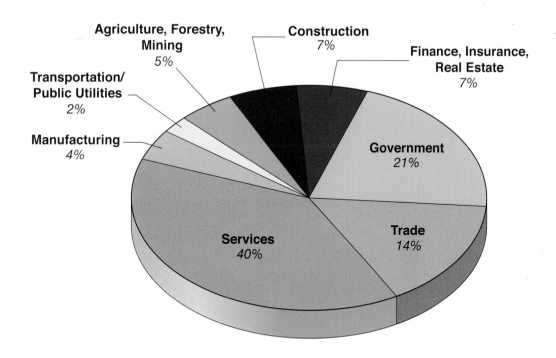

Agriculture, Forestry, Mining
5%

Construction
7%

Finance, Insurance, Real Estate
7%

Transportation/ Public Utilities
2%

Manufacturing
4%

Government
21%

Services
40%

Trade
14%

CHANGING WITH THE TIMES

As New Mexico's economy changes, its cities are forced to change with it. For instance, mining towns are quickly deserted when there is no more ore in the ground. After World War II Madrid, once a thriving coal-mining town, became a ghost town, a jumble of tattered buildings with broken windows. In the early 1970s the coal company that owned all the buildings in town auctioned them off. In just a few days artists and others who wanted to escape to a place where they could live very cheaply bought every building. Today, 80 percent of Madrid's three hundred residents are artists, "a higher percentage than any other town in the country," one resident boasted. It has plenty of art but not one grocery store or supermarket, not one store to buy shoes and socks and underwear, and no gas stations. It also has no local government. This is truly a place for rugged individualists.

Once a mining town, Madrid has transformed itself into an artist community with many studios and galleries.

EARNING A LIVING

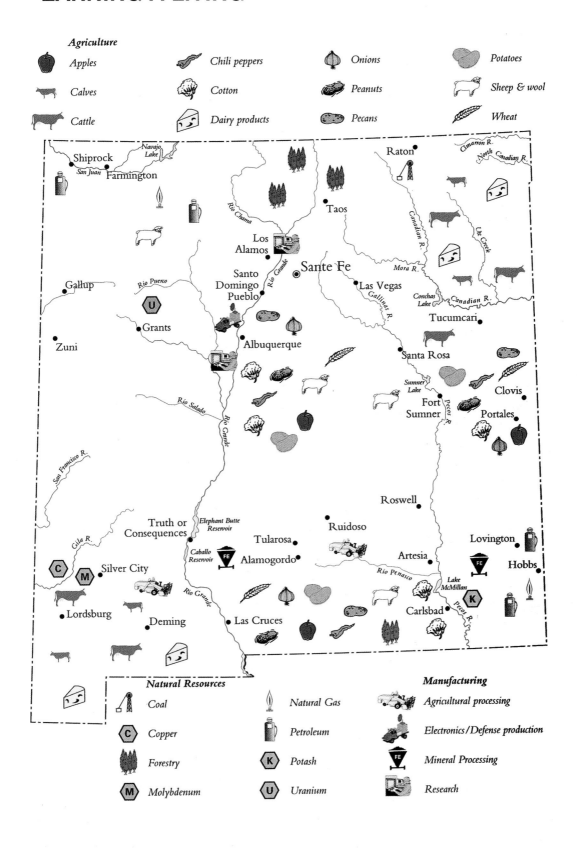

Agriculture

Apples
Calves
Cattle
Chili peppers
Cotton
Dairy products
Onions
Peanuts
Pecans
Potatoes
Sheep & wool
Wheat

Shiprock
Farmington
Navajo Lake
San Juan
Raton
Cimarron R.
North Canadian R.
Rio Chama
Taos
Los Alamos
Santo Domingo Pueblo
Sante Fe
Canadian R.
Las Vegas
Mora R.
Conchas Lake
Canadian R.
Ute Creek
Gallup
Rio Puerco
U
Grants
Zuni
Albuquerque
Gallinas R.
Tucumcari
Santa Rosa
Clovis
Rio Salado
Rio Grande
Sumner Lake
Fort Sumner
Pecos R.
Portales
San Francisco R.
Roswell
Truth or Consequences
Elephant Butte Reservoir
Ruidoso
Lovington
Gila R.
Caballo Reservoir
FE
Alamogordo
Tularosa
Artesia
FE
Hobbs
C
M Silver City
Rio Penasco
Lake McMillan
K
Lordsburg
Deming
Rio Grande
Las Cruces
Carlsbad
Pecos R.

Natural Resources

Coal
Copper
Forestry
Molybdenum
Natural Gas
Petroleum
K Potash
U Uranium

Manufacturing

Agricultural processing
Electronics/Defense production
FE Mineral Processing
Research

The manufacturing of solar panels is a growing industry in New Mexico.

Madrid is not the only place where people live according to their own rules. Many New Mexicans live "off the grid," an expression that means they don't depend on electricity created by power stations for light and heat. Instead they put up solar panels, collect rainwater, and burn wood in stoves. Their goal is to reduce the state's dependence on electricity created by burning fossil fuels and also to reduce their living costs. New Mexico, with its three hundred days of sunshine a year, is an ideal place to harness solar power.

New Mexico has also enjoyed an increase in manufacturing jobs. These range from work in the aviation and bedding products industries to the construction of new buses. Advent Solar plans to add one thousand jobs between 2005 and 2010. Two other firms, Solar Ventures and Solar Torx, broke ground for factories in 2006 and should be producing solar panels by 2008. Once they're up and running, it is believed that enough electricity to power 100,000 average homes will be generated. The particular site, near the town of Deming, was chosen because it receives abundant sunshine and is also close to electrical transmission lines.

Albuquerque is also enjoying a surge in jobs in call centers. One firm, Sento Corporation, added six hundred bilingual employees in 2005. With its large Hispanic population, New Mexico is an ideal place for employers to find bilingual workers. A technical support center was opened by Verizon Wireless at the end of 2006, with eight hundred employees. Another nine hundred workers were added in 2007.

Chapter Six

Out and About in New Mexico

From north to south and east to west New Mexico is chock-full of the gorgeous, the fascinating, and the just plain weird.

THE SOUTH

Deep under southeastern New Mexico lies the state's most famous natural wonder, the Carlsbad Caverns, which is among the world's largest cave systems. The caverns were created over millions of years, as slightly acidic water dripped through cracks in a limestone mountain. Gradually the water wore away the rock, creating large caverns. The seeping water also left behind little bits of minerals. Drop by drop these minerals accumulated into extraordinary formations.

Walking into the Big Room at Carlsbad Caverns is like stepping into a gigantic Dr. Seuss book—it seems too absurd to be natural. Huge, gloopy formations are everywhere. Thin rods called soda straws hang from the

Tourists climb a simple ladder at Alcove House at Bandelier National Monument.

The huge stalagmite Rock of Ages is in the Big Room in Carlsbad Caverns.

ceiling and sometimes have small, round globs called popcorn attached to them. Ripply formations known as draperies are attached to some walls. Even today constant dripping reminds visitors that some of the formations are still changing and growing.

People visit Carlsbad Caverns to see not only the wondrous underground world but also its famous bat colony. Between April and October hundreds of thousands of Mexican free-tailed bats make their home there. Each evening they spiral out of the cave entrance in a huge, swarming tornado and head off for a night of feasting on insects. They return again at dawn, to spend the day sleeping in their favorite cavern.

Most people travel to New Mexico to gaze at wondrous mountains or to explore ancient ruins, but some go to learn about aliens. The most famous alleged UFO sighting in American history occurred near Roswell, and the city has not one but two museums dedicated to UFOs. At the International UFO Museum and Research Center, you might hear a "certified UFO investigator" claim that there are twenty different known species of aliens, some living among us. You can watch videos of people talking about their supposed alien encounters and see photos of fuzzy objects that look like Frisbees. You can also buy lots of souvenirs.

THE ROSWELL INCIDENT

In 1947 a shepherd stumbled across some debris on a ranch outside of Roswell. The U.S. Air Force gathered up the wreckage, examined it, and then issued an extraordinary press release saying that they had found a flying saucer. The news shot around the world. The next day the air force changed their tune—it was a weather balloon, they said. Fifty years later many people still do not believe them.

Not everyone in Roswell is happy about the city's claim to fame. "Some people come up to me and say, 'Gosh, I don't like this. I don't want to be known as the kook capital,'" says local businessman Bill Pope. He reminds Roswell residents that aliens equal money. Says Pope, "There's a little community not far from us over here that has lizard races. What it all comes down to is having something to create an interest in your community. . . . And that creates an inflow of people, and that creates dollars."

Those Roswellians who haven't met any aliens often point to the Roswell Museum and Art Center as the best museum their city has to offer. The museum features an extensive collection of art by New Mexico's painters, potters, and sculptors, along with displays of Spanish armor and Indian artifacts. The museum's highlight is the exhibit devoted to rocket scientist Robert Goddard, who spend much of his career doing experiments nearby. On display are many of his rockets and a replica of his workshop.

West of Roswell you pass through mile upon mile of dry, hilly rangeland before finally climbing into the greenery of the Capitan Mountains. There you will find the tiny town of Lincoln, where Billy the Kid once wreaked havoc. All of Lincoln—it only has one street—is now a state monument, and you can tread the rough floors of the courthouse where the Kid made his violent escape.

Southwest of Lincoln is another of New Mexico's extraordinary natural wonders. White Sands National Monument is 230 square miles of brilliant white sand dunes made of a mineral called gypsum. Near the park's edge, where the dunes are flatter, a few plants and animals manage to eke out an existence. But in the center of the white expanse, where the strong, steady winds sometimes move the dunes 10 feet per year, plants cannot grow fast enough to take root and survive. In some places in the park you can see nothing but the waves of white around you and hear nothing but the wind whistling across the sand. Building sand castles at the monument is out of the question, because there is no water to hold the sand together. But clambering up the steep dunes and running madly back down again offers plenty of fun.

Farther west, in the majestic Gila National Forest, is Gila Cliff Dwellings National Monument. About seven hundred years ago a band of Mogollon built houses in natural caves in a cliff high above a canyon floor. Exploring

Winds that blow the sand at White Sands National Monument whip the dunes into ever-changing shapes.

Caves at Gila Cliffs National Monument were used as homes by the Mogollan seven hundred years ago.

the caves provides a close-up look at the ancient walls the Mogollon built. Soot from their fires still stains the ceilings, and remnants of tools and corncobs lie in corners.

As you come down from the mountains and head north, the land opens up. On the immense empty plains west of Socorro twenty-seven huge dish antennas comprise the world's largest radio telescope, called the Very Large Array (VLA). Each antenna measures 82 feet across and weighs over 200 tons. They pick up radio waves from distant galaxies, which can tell scientists much about the history of the universe. Inside the VLA visitor center, exhibits explain how radio telescopes work and how the antennas are put together. More awe-inspiring is walking to one of the giant antennas and trying to imagine what it is like hearing from the far reaches of the universe.

PLACES TO SEE

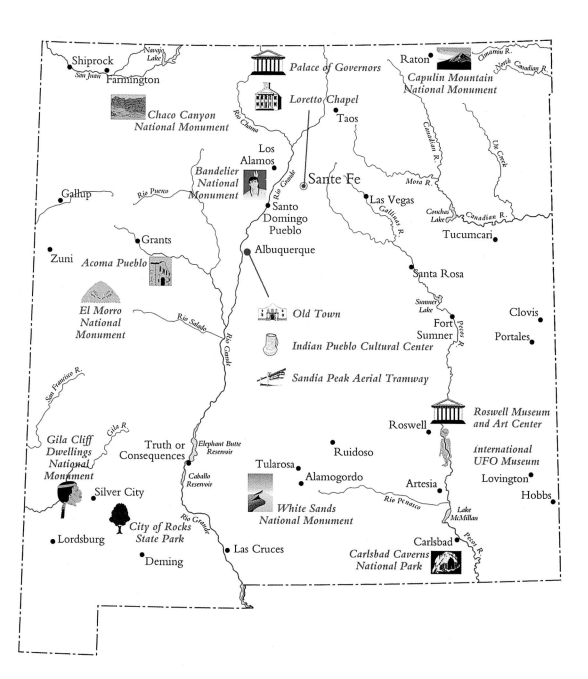

Shiprock

Navajo Lake

San Juan

Farmington

Chaco Canyon National Monument

Palace of Governors

Raton

Cimarron R.

North Canadian R.

Capulin Mountain National Monument

Loretto Chapel

Taos

Rio Chama

Canadian R.

Ute Creek

Los Alamos

Bandelier National Monument

Rio Grande

Sante Fe

Mora R.

Gallup

Rio Puerco

Santo Domingo Pueblo

Las Vegas

Gallinas R.

Conchas Lake

Canadian R.

Grants

Albuquerque

Tucumcari

Zuni

Acoma Pueblo

El Morro National Monument

Rio Salado

Rio Grande

Old Town

Santa Rosa

Summer Lake

Pecos R.

Clovis

Indian Pueblo Cultural Center

Fort Sumner

Portales

Sandia Peak Aerial Tramway

San Francisco R.

Gila R.

Gila Cliff Dwellings National Monument

Truth or Consequences

Elephant Butte Reservoir

Ruidoso

Roswell

Roswell Museum and Art Center

International UFO Museum

Caballo Reservoir

Tularosa

Alamogordo

Artesia

Lovington

Hobbs

Silver City

City of Rocks State Park

White Sands National Monument

Rio Penasco

Lake McMillan

Lordsburg

Rio Grande

Las Cruces

Carlsbad

Pecos R.

Deming

Carlsbad Caverns National Park

The massive bluff called El Morro National Monument provides vivid evidence of New Mexico's long history. A thousand years ago the Anasazi scratched pictures in the rock. In 1605 Juan de Oñate carved a message into the soft sandstone in large, loopy letters. Over the centuries many other explorers, traders, and settlers followed suit, letting the world know that they, too, had stopped at what is now known as Inscription Rock.

The many inscriptions at the base of Inscription Rock were made by the people who passed by it on their travels.

Farther east is Acoma Pueblo. Often called Sky City, Acoma sits atop a massive sandstone rock rising 367 feet above the surrounding plain. This site was once home to 1,500 people, but now only about thirteen families live atop the mesa, which has no running water or electricity. The other Acoma live in modern communities on the valley floor. Historians estimate that the Acoma have been living in Sky City since C.E. 1100, but some people say they have been there since 800. Acoma claims to be the oldest continuously occupied city in the present-day United States. "The people at Hopi Mesa in Arizona and Taos Pueblo will tell you they are the oldest," says the Acoma guide, smiling slyly and wagging his finger. "But don't you believe them. No. Acoma is the oldest." Walking through Acoma's dusty streets, past adobe houses and round stone ovens called *hornos,* the village does seem like it has been there forever.

Acoma Pueblo is built atop a steep 367-foot cliff.

Even more impressive than Acoma's age is its location. Standing at the edge of the rock offers a startling view of the ground far below, other extraordinary rock formations rising from the plain, and white-capped mountains in the distance. It might also offer the chance to look a soaring hawk straight in the eye.

Until a road was built in the 1940s, the Acoma had to carry everything they needed—food, water, building materials, even dirt for their cemetery—up a steep, narrow path of treacherous steps worn into the soft sandstone. Taking this ancient path back down from Acoma, you'll find yourself instinctively reaching for the handholds dug into the walls by countless hands over the centuries.

Albuquerque, New Mexico's largest city by far, spreads out at the base of the Sandia Mountains. Although much of Albuquerque is modern, you can savor the past in Old Town, a pleasant area of narrow streets and small shops surrounding a peaceful plaza. Elsewhere in Albuquerque the Indian Pueblo Cultural Center features displays of jewelry, pottery, and other artifacts from each pueblo. This provides an excellent chance to compare the pottery styles of New Mexico's nineteen pueblos. Every weekend the cultural center hosts traditional dance performances.

For a stunning view, take the Sandia Peak Aerial Tramway, a cable car that quickly rises 4,000 feet from Albuquerque's desert landscape to the chilly pine forests at the top of Sandia Peak. If you're not crazy about heights, you can drive up, too, but it takes much longer. From the top visitors can take in an 11,000-square-mile view that stretches in all directions. Birdlife is plentiful, and visitors may see golden eagles, hawks, and ravens. There are also black bears, raccoons, and bobcats in the mountains.

Each October the Albuquerque International Balloon Fiesta attracts people from far and wide to watch colorful hot-air balloons

Balloons color the landscape during the Albuquerque International Balloon Fiesta.

float gracefully against the brilliant blue sky. This is the world's largest balloon festival and is often touted as the world's most photographed event. More than seven hundred balloons take part.

Albuquerque is uniquely suited for this event, weather-wise. There is a phenomenon here called the Box that makes it possible for a balloon to ascend, float, and then descend back to its launch site. When the balloon lifts up, it finds an air current that carries it along to a certain point. The balloonist can then descend to a lower air current that is blowing in the opposite direction and return to the starting point.

There is no other ballooning location in the world that lets you land where you began.

On October 1, 2005, the Anderson-Abruzzo International Balloon Museum opened on the northern boundary of Albuquerque, next to one of the main balloon-launching sites and with a view of the Sandia Mountains. The museum depicts the history of ballooning and has models of many famous contraptions used in the sport. Visitors can sit in a balloon gondola, the basket that holds travelers, and take a virtual balloon ride.

Most people find little to lure them off the freeway on the long drive from Albuquerque to the Texas border, but the small town of Tucumcari does have one wonderfully weird site that should not be missed. The Tucumcari Historical Research Institute is unlike any other museum you've ever seen. Where else could you find displays of barbed wire, old saddles, bottles, and fishing hats? Housing an amazing jumble of junk—perhaps whatever happened to be in somebody's barn—the museum offers a glimpse of the New Mexico that does not appear in tourist brochures.

THE TURQUOISE TRAIL

Head east of Albuquerque to the little town of Tijeras, and you are at the start of the Turquoise Trail, a 62-mile route that takes in some of the region's most intriguing sites and, of course, its turquoise mines. The mines were centered in and around Cerrillos and date back to 1300, when they were worked by Native Americans. They were followed by Spanish explorers who worked the mines during the seventeenth and eighteenth centuries. The last phase of turquoise mining was in the 1880s, when Anglo miners worked until the mines were exhausted. Today Cerrillos looks like a set for a Western movie. It is home to the

Cerrillos Turquoise Mining Museum, which displays a collection of tools, equipment, and artifacts used by the miners.

TRIBES OF NEW MEXICO

The Navajo Nation is the largest Native-American tribe in the United States. It is found in the Four Corners area, where it occupies parts of northwest New Mexico, northeast Arizona, and a small part of southeast Utah. About 70,000 Navajo live in New Mexico, out of a total Navajo population of more than 250,000.

TEN LARGEST CITIES

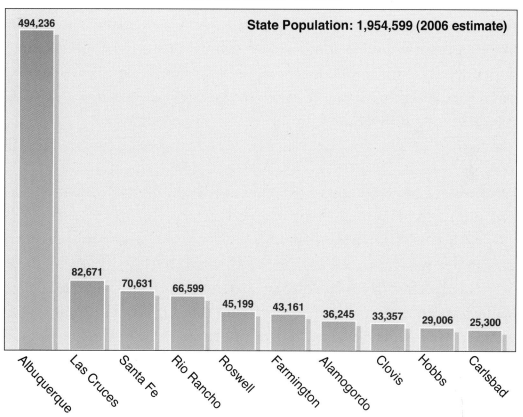

State Population: 1,954,599 (2006 estimate)

City	Population
Albuquerque	494,236
Las Cruces	82,671
Santa Fe	70,631
Rio Rancho	66,599
Roswell	45,199
Farmington	43,161
Alamogordo	36,245
Clovis	33,357
Hobbs	29,006
Carlsbad	25,300

FOUR CORNERS MONUMENT

The extreme northwestern section of New Mexico is part of a unique piece of geography. This is the only place in the United States where four states meet: New Mexico, Arizona, Utah, and Colorado. There is a monument marking the exact spot. When you stand on it, you are actually standing in all four states at the same time. In New Mexico this region is part of the Navajo Nation reservation.

The Pueblo Native Americans, named for the types of homes they build, live in nineteen pueblos and three reservations within New Mexico and are the oldest tribal communities in the United States. All of these areas can be found along a corridor that stretches from Albuquerque in the south to Taos in the north, and few are more than an hour's drive from Albuquerque. Among the well-known pueblos are Acoma, Laguna, Sandia, San Juan, Taos, and Zuni. The three reservations are the Navajo, the Jicarilla Apache, and the Mescalero Apache. These are located to the west of Santa Fe. The Navajo reservation straddles the border with Arizona. Visitors are welcome to visit the pueblos during special ceremonies and dances but are expected to respect the cultural traditions of the Native Americans who live there. They will be rewarded with sights and sounds and smells that are unique in the world.

The Apache Native Americans in New Mexico live on the Jicarilla and Mescalero reservations. There are also Apache living in neighboring Arizona. The Mescalero Apache live in the Sierra Blanca Mountains in southern New Mexico. The tribe was formally recognized by the United States in 1874. The Jicarilla Apache live in the mountains of northern

New Mexico, next to the Colorado border. They were in contact with the Pueblo Native Americans of Taos and Picurís. The Taos Pueblo is a World Heritage Site and is recognized as one of the oldest continually inhabited settlements in the United States.

New Mexico's Native Americans also live in urban communities, including Albuquerque, which is home to thousands of Native Americans. At the Indian Pueblo Cultural Center in the heart of the city, visitors can see Indian dancers and artists at work every weekend. The center is also home to two museums. At the Pueblo House Children's Museum, a "hands-on" facility designed for children from kindergarten through fifth grade, children learn about the rich history, long-lasting culture, and revered traditions of the Pueblo. In the main museum, exhibits trace the Pueblo Indian history and show artifacts that predate the arrival of the Spanish colonists. Dances are held year-round. In the summer months there is an open-air "theater in the round" where visitors can view dancing while they sit on benches. In the cold winter months a 260-seat theater is home to stage presentations.

Zuni dancers perform at the Indian Pueblo Cultural Center in Albuquerque.

When most people think of New Mexico, they think of Santa Fe and its muted adobe buildings nestled in the hills. The heart of Santa Fe is the Plaza, a lovely, grassy square where natives and tourists alike can while away a pleasant afternoon. Santa Fe, the oldest capital city in the United States, is home to the Palace of Governors, the nation's oldest continuously used public building, which was erected in 1610. The palace is now the State History Museum for New Mexico and has exhibits detailing the region's history since the Spaniards arrived. Displays range from a reconstruction of a colonial chapel to unusual frontier objects such as a rawhide violin and a chandelier made from tin cans.

Another Santa Fe highlight is the Loretto Chapel and its famous "miraculous staircase." This elegant spiral staircase, which rises to the choir loft, was built without any nails or central support. The only thing holding it up is the quality of its craftsmanship. According to legend the staircase was built by a traveling carpenter, who disappeared after finishing the job without so much as leaving his name, much less accepting payment.

North of Santa Fe, in Ranchos de Taos, stands one of the most extraordinary buildings in New Mexico. Built in 1730, the church of San Francisco de Asís, with its pure, abstract form, is more sculpture than architecture. Its plain brown adobe walls

The Loretto Chapel in Santa Fe features the "miraculous staircase."

lack the sharp corners and flat surfaces of most buildings. Instead they curve toward the bright blue sky. The fact that they are 4 feet thick and uncluttered by any windows only adds to their power. "One almost shakes in its presence," architectural historian G. E. Kidder once wrote.

Taos Pueblo, another of New Mexico's magnificent architectural accomplishments, lies father north. A sprawling collection of adobe buildings, the pueblo is an endlessly captivating array of angles and corners. The village has sat at the same spot since the 1300s. One Taos Indian says, "The story of my people and the story of this place are one single story. No man can think of us without thinking of this place. We are always joined together."

Not far from Taos, Bandelier National Monument in lovely Frijoles Canyon boasts an impressive group of Anasazi ruins and cave dwellings. The canyon's cliffs are made of volcanic ash. Over the course of hundreds of thousands of years the ash was pressed together into a soft pink and white rock called tuff, which wears away easily. So many holes have developed in the walls of Frijoles Canyon that they look like Swiss cheese. The Anasazi took full advantage of this, hollowing out some of the holes further and building dwellings inside them. On the canyon floor are the ruins of a four-hundred-room village. You can still see the town's central plaza, the round kivas dug into the ground, and remnants of the ancient walls.

Cliff walls at Bandelier National Monument bear scars from erosion.

The most amazing spot at Bandelier is the ceremonial cave, which lies 150 feet above the canyon floor and can only be reached by climbing a series of rough ladders up the cliff wall. Unless you have a strong fear of heights, the climb is well worth the effort. The ceremonial cave is the perfect place to sit, relax, and listen to the wind rustling through the leaves, the birds twittering, and the rain softly falling, and imagine what life was like for the people who lived in this stunning spot centuries ago.

Bandelier is on the eastern edge of the Jemez Mountains, which abound with outdoor activities: fishing for trout in clear streams, hiking through dense pine forests past outcroppings of brilliant red rocks, or simply relaxing in the cool shade of dark green trees. These mountains also offer more exotic surprises. The unusual natural formation called the Soda Dam was created over thousands of years by the buildup of minerals from nearby springs. The weird mushroom-shaped formation now blocks most of the Jemez River, forcing the water to gush through the one tunnel it has eroded in the dam. Although the Soda Dam is fascinating to look at and fun to walk on, you might not want to hang around too long—it smells terrible. The minerals in the dam give it a sulfurous aroma.

A better place to loiter is Spence Hot Springs. A million years ago volcanic explosions created the Jemez Mountains. Today, deep underground, hot pockets still boil and bubble, creating the region's many hot springs. Spence Hot Springs is a beautiful series of pools set among boulders, where the hot water falls from one to another, like a fabulous 104-degree shower. No signs point to Spence Hot Springs, so only people who have been told by someone else know where to pull off the road. Those who find it can lounge in the warm bubbling water and watch the light of day fade, with only the peaceful forest and lovely mountains in view—not a car, a road, or a building in sight.

In New Mexico's northwest corner, down 20 miles of unpaved road that turns to impassable mud with the coming of rain, lies Chaco Canyon, the site of the Anasazi's greatest achievement. Chaco Canyon was a political, religious, and trade center for the Anasazi. Perfectly straight roads, some 30 feet wide, extended to communities as far as 42 miles away. No one knows why the Anasazi put so much effort into building the roads, since they had no carts or other vehicles that required them. Between C.E. 900 and 1200 the Anasazi built great apartment buildings at Chaco. The largest of these, Pueblo Bonito, contained more than six hundred rooms. As many as five thousand people lived at Chaco, making it the largest settlement in what is now the United States prior to the arrival of Europeans.

Although the Anasazi are long gone, the ruins of their incredible buildings remain. Wandering through Chaco Canyon, the first thing that strikes you is the sheer size of the structures. On closer inspection you may notice that Anasazi masonry is extraordinary. Beauty seemed to be almost as important to the Anasazi as function, for they put the rocks together in careful patterns.

Chaco Canyon is scrubby, high desert punctuated by rocky mesas. Looking out over the barren landscape, it is hard to understand why the Anasazi didn't choose somewhere more welcoming—somewhere with water and trees—for their most elaborate city. Why did the Anasazi choose this site, and why did they abandon it? Mysteries such as these reawaken your sense of New Mexico as a Land of Enchantment.

Built by the Anasazi between 900 C.E. and 1200 C.E., Pueblo Bonito contains more than six hundred rooms.

THE FLAG: The flag shows a red Zia Indian sun symbol—a circle with four radiating points—on a field of yellow. It was adopted in 1925.

THE SEAL: In the center of the seal are two eagles. The larger American bald eagle, with arrows clutched in its talons, protects the smaller Mexican eagle. Underneath is a scroll with the state motto. The seal was adopted in 1912.

State Survey

Statehood: January 6, 1912

Origin of Name: Spanish explorers considered the region part of Mexico

Nickname: Land of Enchantment

Capital: Santa Fe

Motto: *Crescit Eundo* (Grows as It Goes)

Bird: Roadrunner

Mammal: Black bear

Fish: New Mexico cutthroat trout

Insect: Tarantula hawk wasp

Flower: Yucca

Tree: Piñon

Vegetables: Chilies and pinto beans

Grass: Blue gramma

Gem: Turquoise

Black bear

Yucca

O, FAIR NEW MEXICO

In 1915 Elizabeth Garrett, the blind daughter of famed sheriff Pat Garrett, wrote this song, which was adopted as the official state song in 1917. New Mexico also has a state song in Spanish, "Así Es Nuevo

Words & Music by
Elizabeth Garrett

Un - der a sky of az- ure, Where balm-y breez - es

blow; Kissed by the gold - en sun - shine,

Is Nu - e - vo Me- ji - co. Home of the Mon - te -

zu - ma, With fier-y heart a - glow.

State of the deeds his - tor- ic, Is Nue-vo Me - ji -

Méjico," adopted in 1971; a state ballad, "Land of Enchantment," adopted in 1989; and a state poem, "A Nuevo Mexico" ("To New Mexico"), written in 1911 and adopted in 1991.

GEOGRAPHY

Highest Point: 13,161 feet, at Wheeler Peak in Taos County

Lowest Point: 2,817 feet, at Red Bluff Reservoir in Eddy County

Area: 121,590 square miles

Greatest Distance North to South: 395 miles

Great Distance East to West: 355 miles

Bordering States: Colorado to the north, Oklahoma to the east, Texas to the east and south, and Arizona to the west

Hottest Recorded Temperature: 116 ºF at Artesia on June 29, 1918, and at Orogrande on July 14, 1934

Coldest Recorded Temperature: –50 ºF at Gavilan on February 1, 1951

Most Snowfall in a Single Storm: 78 inches at Anchor Mine, December 1–5, 1913

Average Annual Precipitation: 13 inches

Major Rivers: Canadian, Gila, Pecos, Rio Grande, San Juan

Major Lakes: Bottomless Lake, Conchas Reservoir, Elephant Butte Reservoir, Lake Sumner, Navajo Reservoir

Trees: blue spruce, desert willow, Douglas fir, juniper, piñon, ponderosa pine, Rio Grande cottonwood

Wild Plants: creosote bush, desert marigold, desert zinnia, fishhook barrel cactus, mesquite, sunset cactus, yucca

Animals: antelope, Barbary sheep, bighorn sheep, bobcat, black bear, coyote, elk, fox, jackrabbit, lizard, mink, mountain lion, mule deer, muskrat, prairie dog, rattlesnake

Birds: crane, duck, hawk, heron, hummingbird, owl, pelican, roadrunner, sandpiper, tern, wild turkey, woodpecker

Fish: bass, bream, catfish, crappie, perch, pike, trout

Endangered Animals: American peregrine falcon, bald eagle, Gila trout, least tern, Mexican long-nosed bat, Mexican spotted owl, New Mexican ridge-nosed rattlesnake, Southwestern willow flycatcher, whooping crane

Mexican spotted owl

Endangered Plants: gypsum wild-buckwheat, Knowlton cactus, Kuenzler hedgehog cactus, Lee pincushion cactus, Lloyd's hedgehog cactus, Lloyd's mariposa cactus, Mesa Verde cactus, Sacramento Mountains thistle, Sacramento prickly-poppy, Sneed pincushion cactus

TIMELINE

New Mexico History

C.E. 900–1300 The Anasazi build a network of hundreds of stone buildings in Chaco Canyon.

1200–1500 Pueblo Native Americans establish villages along the Rio Grande.

1536 Alvar Núñez Cabeza de Vaca, Estéban the Moor, and two others possibly cross what is now southern New Mexico before arriving in Mexico.

1540–1542 Francisco Vásquez de Coronado explores the area from the Gulf of California to present-day Kansas, including New Mexico.

1598 Juan de Oñate establishes San Juan de los Caballeros, the first Spanish colony in New Mexico.

1609–1610 Gaspar de Villagra publishes an epic history of the founding of New Mexico, the first book printed about any area in the United States.

1680 The Pueblo Indian revolt expels all Spaniards from New Mexico.

1692 Don Diego de Vargas reconquers New Mexico for Spain.

1706 Albuquerque is founded.

1776 Franciscan friars Dominquez and Escanté explore the route from New Mexico to California.

1807 Zebulon Pike leads the first Anglo-American expedition into New Mexico.

1821 Mexico declares its independence from Spain; the Santa Fe Trail opens.

1846 The Mexican-American War begins; Stephen Watts Kearney annexes New Mexico to the United States.

1848 The Treaty of Guadalupe Hidalgo ends the Mexican-American War.

1850 New Mexico, which included present-day Arizona, southern Colorado, southern Utah, and southern Nevada, is designated a U.S. territory.

1851 Bishop Jean Baptiste Lamy arrives in New Mexico and establishes schools, hospitals, and orphanages throughout the territory.

1853 The Gadsden Purchase from Mexico adds 45,000 square miles to the territory.

1861 After the outbreak of the Civil War, Confederates invade New Mexico from Texas and declare the Confederate Territory of Arizona.

1862 Union troops twice defeat Confederates, ending the Confederate occupation of New Mexico.

1862–1866 Navajo and Apache are relocated by U.S. government to Bosque Redondo Reservation; thousands die of disease and starvation.

1879 The Atlantic & Pacific Railroad (later renamed the Santa Fe Railroad) arrives in New Mexico, opening full-scale trade and allowing the mass migration of settlers from the East and Midwest.

1881 Billy the Kid is killed by Sheriff Pat Garrett.

1886 The Apache leader Geronimo surrenders, ending Indian hostilities in the Southwest.

1912 New Mexico becomes the forty-seventh state.

1916 The Mexican revolutionary Pancho Villa raids Columbus, New Mexico.

1917 Socialite Mabel Dodge Luhan invites artists such as Ansel Adams and Georgia O'Keeffe to Taos, which becomes known as an artists' haven.

1923 Oil is discovered on the Navajo reservation.

1942 Los Alamos is selected as the secret site for the development of the atomic bomb.

1945 The world's first atomic bomb is detonated in southern New Mexico.

1948 Native Americans win the right to vote in state elections.

1966 The new state capitol is dedicated.

1982 The space shuttle *Columbia* lands at White Sands Space Harbor.

1998 New Mexico celebrates the four-hundredth anniversary of the founding of the first Spanish colony in the region.

2006 Albuquerque celebrates the three-hundredth anniversary of its founding.

ECONOMY

Agricultural Products: cattle, chilies, corn, cotton, hay, milk, onions, pecans, poultry, sheep, wheat, wood

Manufactured Products: communication equipment, construction materials, electronic components, processed foods, refined petroleum, precision instruments

Natural Resources: copper, gold, iron ore, lead, manganese, molybdenum, natural gas, oil, potash, sand and gravel, silver, uranium, zinc

Business and Trade: banking, processed natural resources, real estate, research, tourism

Chilies

CALENDAR OF CELEBRATIONS

New Year's Day Celebration A mass, procession, and traditional dances such as the Turtle and Matachines celebrate the beginning of a new year at Picurís Pueblo, south of Taos.

Mardi Gras in the Mountains This celebration is held in the Red River Ski Basin from late February until early March. It features parades on the ski slopes, balls in the lodges, winter cookouts, snow-sculpture competitions, and sled rides for families.

Chama Winter Carnival The winter carnival in Chama in late February and early March includes snowmobile races, dances, and cross-country ski competitions.

Dinosaur Days In mid-April an open-air bazaar in Clayton includes an Old Western Dance, complete with costumes and prizes. Visitors can also take free tours of prehistoric dinosaur tracks in Clayton Lake State Park.

Taos Spring Arts Festival This May festival in Taos includes an arts-and-crafts show and many gallery openings and museums exhibitions.

Las Vegas Rails 'n' Trails Days Each June a fiddlers' contest, barbecue, rodeo, and country-and-western dancing event commemorate the historic Santa Fe Trail and the arrival of the railroad in Las Vegas.

Clovis Music Festival Rock 'n' roll greats such as Buddy Holly and Roy Orbison recorded their hits at Norman Petty's recording studio in Clovis. This festival, held in mid-July, celebrates the music of the 1950s with outdoor dances, an antique auto show, and live music performances.

San Juan County Fair Farmington is the site of the largest county fair in New Mexico each August. This weeklong event features concerts, livestock shows, exhibits, a fiddling contest, a parade, an arts-and-crafts show, and a carnival.

Intertribal Indian Ceremonial In late August New Mexico's oldest all-Indian exhibition attracts tribe members and visitors from across the United States, Canada, and Mexico to a powwow, rodeo, Indian arts-and-crafts show, and parade in Gallup.

Mountain Man Rendezvous and Buffalo Roast The rough-and-tumble life of mountain men is the theme of this Santa Fe event in late August. It features traditional music, blacksmithing, tomahawk throwing, and a mountain man's dinner, featuring wild game dishes such as rattlesnake, elk, rabbit, grouse, deer, and buffalo.

Santa Fe Indian Market First held in 1922, this August exhibition of Native American art is the oldest and largest in the world. Displays include handmade baskets, pottery, rugs, jewelry, drums, kachina dolls, sandpainting, and much more.

Fiesta de Santa Fe The oldest community festival in the nation commemorates the reconquest of New Mexico by Don Diego de Vargas in 1692. The pageantry includes the arrival of the Fiesta Queen and her court, reenactments of Don Diego's arrival in Santa Fe, and the burning of Zozobra (Old Man Gloom). The fiesta is held the weekend after Labor Day.

Staked Plains Roundup Horse lovers will enjoy the cowboy poetry, western music, saddle making, boot making, blacksmithing, rawhide braiding, and horse shows at this event held near Hobbs in late September.

Rodeo

Albuquerque International Balloon Fiesta Each October Albuquerque hosts the world's biggest fiesta, which features hundreds of hot-air balloons. Although not a race, prizes are awarded to balloonists who can land closest to target areas or snatch objects off the ground while in low flight.

Cloudcroft Oktoberfest Hayrides, food booths, square dances, nature tours, a horseshoe tournament, and an art competition are some of the attractions at this October event in Cloudcroft.

Festival of the Cranes This November event celebrates the return of tens of thousands of sandhill cranes, along with other bird species, including snow geese, bald eagles, wild turkeys, and whooping cranes, to the Bosque del Apache National Wildlife Refuge in San Antonio for the winter. There are workshops, tours, and children's events such as nature walks, films, and puppet shows.

Indian National Finals Rodeo The best Native American rodeo riders from the United States and Canada compete for the title of World Champion Indian Cowboy in mid-November in Albuquerque.

Shalako Ceremony and Dance In early December six 10-foot-tall masked dancers wearing colorful costumes begin a nightlong house-blessing ceremony by crossing a small river that runs through Zuñi Pueblo. Visitors from around the world come to see this solemn event.

Christmas at the Palace The Governor's Palace in Santa Fe is the site of traditional holiday festivities in mid-December, including storytelling, candle lighting, music playing, and the serving of *bizcochitos*, coffee, and cider.

Albuquerque International Balloon Fiesta

Rudolfo Anaya (1937–) was born in Pastura and became a teacher and school counselor before turning to writing. His novels *Bless Me, Ultima* and *Tortuga*, which draw heavily on his Latino heritage, have won many awards.

Rudolfo Anaya

William H. Bonney (1859?–1881), who was better known as Billy the Kid, was born in New York and came to New Mexico as a child. As a teenager he became a gambler, a killer, and a ringleader in the cattle wars between ranchers. When Bonney escaped from prison after being convicted of murder, Sheriff Pat Garrett tracked him down and shot him dead in Fort Sumner.

Fernando E. Cabeza de Baca (1937–), born in Albuquerque, is a direct descendant of the Spanish explorer of the same name. He served in the army during the Vietnam War and then was appointed a special assistant by President Gerald Ford in 1974, making him the youngest and highest-ranking federal executive of Hispanic descent.

Kit Carson (1809–1868) ran away from his home in Missouri at age sixteen and became a trapper and trader along the Santa Fe Trail. He was also an Indian fighter who forced the Navajo across New Mexico in the Long Walk. He was a frontier hero and a legend in his day.

Willa Cather (1873–1947) was
living in New Mexico, looking for
subjects for her stories, when she
learned how Bishop Lamy had
built schools and orphanages in
New Mexico. His life gave her
the idea for a novel that became
an American classic, *Death
Comes for the Archbishop*. Cather
was born in Winchester, Virginia.

Willa Cather

John Simpson Chisum (1824–1884)
was the first cattle rancher in New
Mexico. Moving his cattle operation from Texas, Chisum settled
permanently at South Spring, near
Roswell. When the cattle wars
broke out, he led the movement
to restore law and order, hiring Sheriff Pat Garrett to hunt down
Billy the Kid. Chisum afterward became known as the Cattle King.

John Denver (1943–1997) started out as a folksinger with the Chad
Mitchell Trio. After going solo in 1968, he composed and recorded a
number of hits, including "Leaving on a Jet Plane," "Rocky Mountain High," and "Annie's Song." He was active in many causes,
including UNICEF, Friends of the Earth, and Save the Children.
Denver was born in Roswell.

Max Evans (1925–) is rated number eleven on the Western Writers of America's list of the best western authors of the twentieth century. This Albuquerque resident captures the vanishing West in his books. One of his recent books, *Making a Hand: Growing Up Cowboy in New Mexico*, depicts the education of boys and girls learning the skills of "cowboying," a disappearing vocation.

Greer Garson (1908–1996) emigrated from Ireland and made her reputation in Hollywood as a leading lady in films such as *Mrs. Miniver*, *Random Harvest*, and *Madame Curie*. She was nominated for the Oscar every year between 1941 and 1945. She eventually retired to New Mexico, where she and her husband became involved in environmental causes, donating hundreds of acres of their property to the state park system.

R. C. Gorman (1932–2005) was an internationally known Navajo artist. His most popular works are lithographs, woodblocks, and charcoal portrayals of people often caught in reflective moments and in natural settings. In 1973 he became the first living Native-American artist to have his work on permanent display

R. C. Gorman

in the Metropolitan Museum of Art in New York City. His father, Carl Nelson Gorman, was one of the Navajo code talkers of World War II.

Tony Hillerman (1925–) is the author of more than fifteen best-selling mystery novels that concentrate on the clash between modern society and traditional Navajo values and customs. His novels, such as *Skinwalkers* and *Talking God*, display a deep understanding of Navajo culture. Hillerman lives in Albuquerque.

Conrad Hilton (1887–1979), who was born in San Antonio, New Mexico, helped run his father's businesses, which included renting rooms to migrant workers. After serving in World War I, Hilton invested in a small hotel. By the 1960s his Hilton hotel chain was one of the largest chains of luxury hotels in the world. He told his story in a popular book about putting customers first, *Be My Guest*.

Dolores Huerta (1930–), a labor organizer, was born in Dawson, a small mining town in northern New Mexico. Her mother ran a boardinghouse for migrant workers. Later Huerta joined Cesar Chávez in building the National Farm Workers Association (now called the United Farm Workers of America), which waged a difficult but ultimately successful campaign to improve the working conditions of migrant workers in the Southwest.

Jean Baptiste Lamy (1814–1888), a Catholic bishop born in France, was sent by the Vatican to Santa Fe in 1851. He arrived to find fourteen priests serving a region sprawled over five states. He built schools, hospitals, and churches. His work was the basis for Willa Cather's novel *Death Comes for the Archbishop*.

Nancy Lopez (1957–), one of the best golfers ever, moved to Roswell from Torrance, California, as a young girl. Her parents, avid golfers, taught her to play. She developed into a record-breaking professional golfer, winning two national amateur championships and forty-eight professional golf tournaments. Lopez was inducted into the Ladies Professional Golf Hall of Fame in 1987, when she was thirty years old.

Manuelito (1818–1893) was a Navajo leader who led an attack on Fort Defiance in Arizona. Later he successfully persuaded federal authorities to allow the Navajo to return to their homeland after the Long Walk to Bosque Redondo Reservation.

Maria Martinez (1887–1980) was a leading Native American artist. Born in San Ildefonso Pueblo, near Santa Fe, she made her first pottery as a child of seven or eight. Her elegant black-on-black pottery earned her worldwide renown.

Bill Mauldin (1921–2003) a cartoonist, was born in Mountain Park. While serving in World War II, he drew cartoons about the true lives of battle-weary soldiers, which later appeared in St. Louis and Chicago newspapers. He won the Pulitzer Prize in 1945 and 1959.

N. Scott Momaday (1934–) writes poetry and fiction that reflect his Kiowa Indian heritage. He was born in Oklahoma, moved to Jemez Pueblo when he was twelve, and later attended the University of New Mexico. His Pulitzer Prize–winning novel, *House Made of Dawn*, is about the overlap of Indian and Anglo cultures.

Nancy Lopez

Demi Moore (1962–), the star of movies such as *Ghost, A Few Good Men*, and *G.I. Jane*, was born in Roswell. After starting out in television on *General Hospital*, Moore became a major Hollywood actress in a few short years.

John Nichols (1940–) was born in Berkeley, California. At age sixteen, he got off a Greyhound bus in Taos and decided to stay. His New Mexican trilogy of novels, *The Milagro Beanfield War, The Magic Journey*, and *The Nirvana Blues*, is about the destruction of old cultures in the name of progress.

Georgia O'Keeffe (1887–1986), an artist, visited New Mexico in 1929, was enraptured, and spent much of the rest of her life there. She often looked to the desert for inspiration for her paintings, which usually featured bold, simplified images of objects from nature. Her works are displayed in museums all over the world.

Bobby Unser (1934–) and **Al Unser** (1939–), both born in Albuquerque, are the best-known members of a famous auto-racing family. Al Unser won the Indianapolis 500 four times; Bobby won it three times. The Unser Racing Museum, which opened in 2005, covers the family's racing history.

Pablita Velarde (1918–2006), an artist, was born at Santa Clara Pueblo. She used natural pigments from the earth in her paintings, grinding them into powders. She has been called the mother of Pueblo painting, because she introduced it to the world.

Demi Moore

Lew Wallace (1827–1905) was a lawyer and a major general in the Civil War before becoming governor of the New Mexico Territory. During his time as governor he put an end to the cattle wars and wrote *Ben Hur*, a popular novel about Christians in ancient Rome.

TOUR THE STATE

Albuquerque Museum of Art, History, and Science (Albuquerque) This museum houses artifacts from 20,000 B.C.E. to the present, including Spanish colonial items and, Native American arts, costumes, photographs, and crafts. The museum also has a special children's section, a library, and a sculpture garden.

Aztec Museum and Pioneer Village (Aztec) Step back in time by visiting a sheriff's office, jail, law office, doctor's office, blacksmith shop, and log cabin, all from around 1880. Museum displays include clocks, dolls, quilts, farm equipment, and other items used by pioneers.

Blue Hole (Santa Rosa) Fed by an underground river, this 81-foot-deep pool near Santa Rosa has crystal clear waters that remain a cool 61°F throughout the year. It attracts diving enthusiasts from all over the world.

Bosque del Apache (Socorro) This 57,000-acre national wildlife refuge along the Rio Grande is home to nearly three hundred species of birds. The birds either live at the refuge or, like the endangered whooping crane, migrate through it on a seasonal basis.

Bradbury Science Museum (Los Alamos) This museum details the secret development of the first atomic bomb. It also features exhibits about defense weapons, energy, and current scientific research.

Carlsbad Caverns National Park (Carlsbad) Twenty miles south of Carlsbad are some of the world's largest limestone caverns. The park preserves a network of eighty caves, some hundreds of feet deep. A colony of hundreds of thousands of Mexican free-tailed bats lives in the caverns.

The Catwalk (Glenwood) Twenty-five feet above tumbling Whitewater Creek in Gila National Forest, a metal walkway clings to the canyon walls. The sheer 250-foot bluffs seem to touch high above. Visitors enjoy hiking and picnicking along this colorful canyon.

Chaco Canyon National Historical Park (Bloomfield) Chaco Canyon preserves the ruins of hundreds of stone buildings, some four stories high, in what was the largest Anasazi settlement.

El Morro National Monument (Grants) Carved on this 200-foot-high sandstone wall are pictures by prehistoric Native Americans, brave words by Spanish explorers, and autographs of westbound pioneers. You can walk around the rock and see the centuries roll past.

Fort Sumner (Fort Sumner) This former military post served as a holding camp for thousands of Navajo during the 1860s, after they were forced to leave their homeland on the Long Walk. It is also the site of Billy the Kid's grave.

Gila Cliff Dwellings National Monument (Silver City) About seven hundred years ago members of the Mogollon culture built homes in natural caves in a canyon wall 200 feet about the Gila River. Archaeologists have unearthed bowls, tools, and artwork in the forty-two rooms made of adobe brick.

International Space Hall of Fame (Alamogordo) This four-story golden cube contains exhibits about space exploration, from the earliest days of rocketry to the present. Highlights include hands-on exhibits about piloting spacecraft and the effects of weightlessness, a simulated walk on Mars, and a collection of video interviews with scientists and astronauts.

International UFO Museum and Research Center (Roswell) Visitors to this museum can learn about alleged UFO sightings and the rumor that an alien spacecraft crashed nearby in 1947. Exhibits show documents claiming that the U.S. military covered up the crash and secretly examined the bodies of aliens recovered at the site.

Las Cruces Museum of Natural History (Las Cruces) Dinosaur bones, fossilized trees, animal skeletons, and gems are all part of this museum dedicated to New Mexico's prehistoric past. The museum also hosts field trips to dig sites.

Rio Grande Zoological Park (Albuquerque) At this zoo visitors can see more than a thousand animals in displays that simulate their natural habitats, including an African savanna and a rain forest. The park also houses a children's zoo and offers educational programs.

Shiprock (Shiprock) A vertical shaft of rock that rises 1,500 feet above the desert floor, Shiprock is called Tse Be dahi (Winged Rock) in the Navajo language. Legend says this sacred landmark, 12 miles southwest of the town of Shiprock, once sprouted wings to carry the Navajo people to safety following an enemy attack.

Smokey Bear Historical State Park (Capitan) Smokey Bear was a real cub rescued from a forest fire near Capitan. The park's visitor center has exhibits about forest fires and fire prevention. Nearby is the grave of Smokey Bear.

Shiprock

Very Large Array (Socorro) The Very Large Array is the world's most powerful radio telescope. The array is used by scientists from all over the world to examine deep space. The site was used in the films *Independence Day* and *Contact*. Self-guided tours are available.

War Eagles Museum (Santa Teresa) This museum displays fighter planes from World War II, jet fighters from the Korean War, and antique automobiles.

FUN FACTS

More painters, sculptors, poets, musicians, dancers, and filmmakers live in north-central New Mexico than in any other area of roughly the same size in the United States.

Constructed in 1610, the Governor's Palace in Santa Fe is the oldest continuously occupied public building in the United States. It has been the home of Spanish and Mexican governors, as well as headquarters for Pueblo Native Americans, the U.S. Army, and the Confederate army. Currently the palace houses a museum.

El Camino Real (the Royal Road), which ran from Mexico City to Santa Fe, was the first road established by Europeans in the present-day United States. Travelers began using it in about 1581.

Find Out More

If you want to learn more about New Mexico, check your local library, bookstore, or video store for these titles:

GENERAL INTEREST BOOKS

Chávez, Thomas E. *New Mexico Past and Future*. Albuquerque: University of New Mexico Press, 2006.

Evans, Max. *Making a Hand: Growing Up Cowboy in New Mexico*. Santa Fe: Museum of New Mexico Press, 2005.

Foote, Cheryl J. *Women of the New Mexico Frontier, 1846–1912*. Albuquerque: University of New Mexico Press, 2005.

Jameson, W. C. *New Mexico Treasure Tales*. Caldwell, ID: Caxton Press, 2003.

FICTION

Robison, Dan. *Wind Seer: The Story of One Native American Boy's Contribution to the Anasazi Culture*. Spokane, WA: Marquette Books, 2005.

VIDEOS

History's Mysteries—Roswell Secrets Unveiled, History Channel, A&E Home Video, 2006.

WEB SITES

New Mexico

http://www.newmexico.org

The New Mexico Department of Tourism site offers plenty of information on what to see and do in the state.

Culture of New Mexico

http://www.nmculturenet.org

This Web site promotes the understanding and appreciation of the diverse cultures of the state.

Land of Enchantment

http://www.kidskonnect.com/NewMexico/NewMexicoHome.html

This site features links that let you explore the history and culture of New Mexico.

Index

Page numbers in **boldface** are illustrations and charts.

Melissa McDaniel is the author of several books for young people. She loves driving through New Mexico's striking landscape, where her travels have taken her from the depths of Carlsbad Caverns to the peaks of the Jemez Mountains.

Ettagale Blauer is an award-winning author with more than twenty-five books to her credit. She frequently writes for young adults on countries and cultures and is also known for her writing on crafts and jewelry. During her most recent trip to New Mexico, she says, "I was reminded of the incredible beauty of this state and the importance of the Native-American culture in the Southwest. I understand why so many artists make this their home." She travels frequently from her home base in New York City.

Jason Lauré is an award-winning photojournalist whose photographs have appeared in more than one hundred books and magazines. He travels the world, photographing cultures, with a special emphasis on children and teens. When he returned to New Mexico in 2006, he found the vitality and beauty of its cultures fascinating. "The whole feeling of the state, the natural beauty and the dynamic culture of the Native Americans, makes it a special place to visit," he says. He divides his year between New York City and Cape Town, South Africa.